# Norfolk the County of my Birth - 3rd Edition

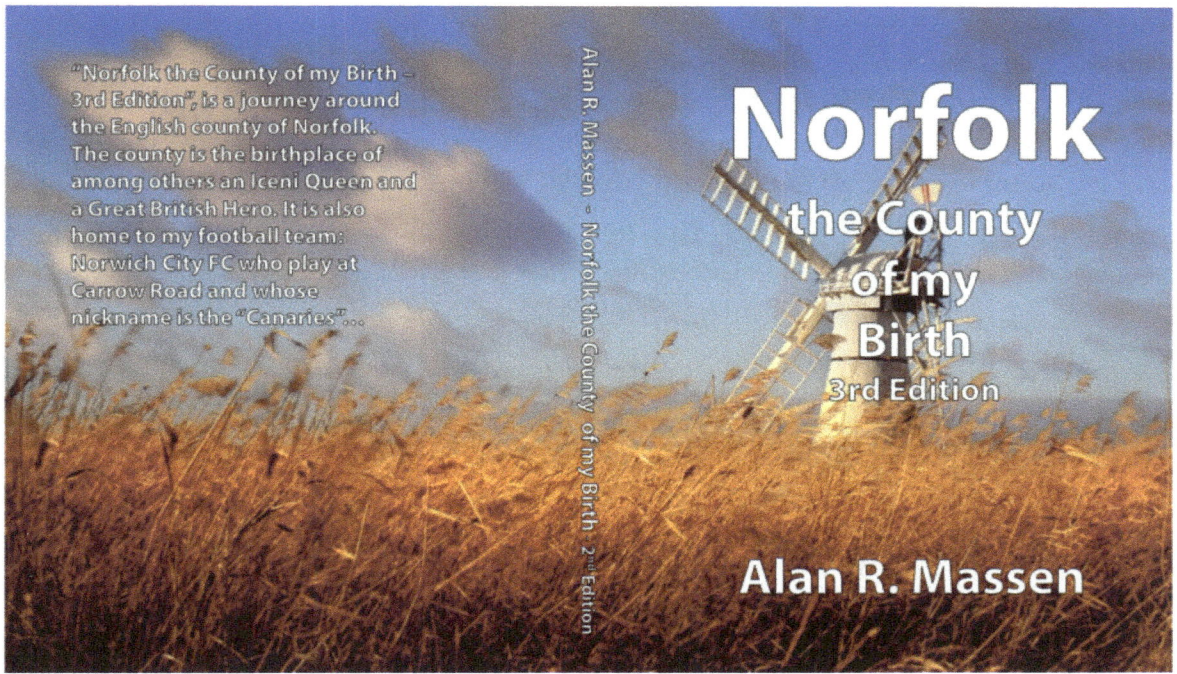

The story in words and pictures of Norfolk the County of my Birth.

by Norfolk Watercolour Artist - Alan R. Massen

Published in Great Britain by Rainbow Publications UK

First Published in 2016 by Rainbow Publications UK
2nd Edition Published in 2019 by Rainbow Publications UK
3rd Edition Published in 2020 by Rainbow Publications UK

Copyright © 2020 Alan R. Massen

The moral right of Alan R. Massen to be identified as the author of this work has been asserted in accordance with the UK Copyright, Designs and Patents Act of 1988.
All rights reserved. No part of this book may be reproduced, or stored in a retrieval system, or transmitted in any form or by any means, electronic, mechanical, photocopying, recording, or otherwise, without the prior written permission of both the author and the above publisher of this book All imagery and illustrations

© Alan R. Massen

Neither the publisher nor the author can accept liability for the use of any of the materials, methods or information recommended in this book or for any consequences arising out of their use, nor can they be held responsible for any errors or omissions that may be found in the text or may occur at a future date as a result of changes in rules, laws or equipment All manufacturers, sellers, product names and services identified in this book are used in editorial fashion and for the benefit of such companies with no intention of any infringement of trademarks. No such use or the use of any trade name is intended to convey endorsement or other affiliation with this book. Every effort has been made to obtain the necessary permissions with reference to copyright material, both illustrative and quoted. We apologize for any omissions in this respect and will be pleased to make the appropriate acknowledgements in any future edition.

Paperback Edition ISBN 978-0-9933962-4-3

Typeset in Minion Pro
Published in Great Britain by Rainbow Publications UK

# About the Author

Alan was born in the city of Norwich in the county of Norfolk, England in November 1949. When Alan was still a teenager he started painting whilst attending art classes in Norwich. In his mid-teens he had two paintings accepted for a National Art Exhibition held in London and other major UK cities. Alan spent most of his working life as a professional Health and Safety Advisor and rarely picked up a paint brush until he, his wife Susie and daughter Ginny (his other daughter Mandy is married and lives with her husband Adrian in Sheffield) moved out of the city of Norwich into the countryside in 1993. They moved to a little village called East Lexham in the heart of Norfolk. The village was very peaceful and pretty. This helped inspire Alan to take up watercolour painting once again. In 2004 they moved to another small West Norfolk village near Downham Market where they still live today. In 2008 Alan had to retire due to ill health (bad knees). He continued to paint in watercolours regularly and also started writing. He has had forty six books published to-date. In 2019 he produced this Book that showcases Norfolk the County of his birth.

# Dedication

I would like to dedicate this book, to orthopaedic surgeon Mr. James Jeffery and I would also like to acknowledge our friends Andy, Lynn, Corri, Alistair, Issy, Karl, Anna and all our Greek friends at the Troulos Bay Hotel and at the Mythos Cafe on the Greek Paradise Island of Skiathos for all their friendship over the many years we have visited there. A very special thank you must go to my wife Susie who helps and supports me in all I do every single day of my life. I love you all to the moon and back!

# Books by the Author

- Retiring to our Garden Year One
- Retiring to our Garden Year Two
- Retiring into a Rainbow
- Retiring into a Rainbow 2nd Edition
- Skiathos a Greek Island Paradise
- Norfolk the County of my Birth 2nd Edition
- Art Inspired by a Rainbow
- Ibiza Island of Dreams
- Majorca Island in the Sun
- Flip-Flops and Shades on Thassos
- Mardle and a Troshin' in Norfolk
- England the Country of my Birth
- Mousehole the Cornish Jewel
- Sunshades and Flip-Flops on Kefalonia
- Shades and Flip-Flops on Zakynthos
- Trips into my Mind's Eye 2nd Edition
- Corfu and Mainland Greece
- Crete and the Island of Santorini
- Cyprus, the Pyramids and the Holy Land
- Greek Islands in the Sun
- Trips into My Mind's Eye
- Norfolk the County of my Birth
- Being Greek "The Culture of the People of Greece"

Copyright © 2020 Alan R. Massen
I hope you enjoy this my latest book featuring my home County of **NORFOLK**…

# Contents

| | |
|---|---|
| Introduction | 1 |
| The History of Norfolk | 11 |
| The Norfolk Coast | 31 |
| Out and About in Norfolk | 53 |
| Norfolk in Black and White | 76 |
| My Norfolk | 84 |
| My Memories of Norfolk | 134 |
| My Village | 141 |
| Norfolk Wildlife | 153 |
| Norfolk in Colour | 185 |
| Our Norfolk Snaps | 205 |
| Acknowledgements | 226 |

Copyright © 2020 Alan R. Massen

# Introduction

Alan, Susie and family members on our patio enjoying some good company, good food, fine wine in the warm Norfolk sunshine

"Norfolk the County of my Birth", is a journey around the English county of Norfolk. The county is the birthplace of among others an Iceni Queen and a Great British Hero. It is also home to my football team: Norwich City FC who play at Carrow Road and whose nickname is the "Canaries". This is the 46th book that I have had published. I have written about my garden, my watercolour paintings, English history, The County of Norfolk, the Paradise Greek Island of Skiathos and much, much more. In this book we are focusing on the county of my birth Norfolk. The book also contains examples of my artwork and our photographs. These have been produced by scanning my watercolour paintings and photographs onto my computer and then using a piece of art software that gives them an Impressionist effect…a bit like Claude Monet. I will also include some of my recollections and memories of living and travelling around the County of Norfolk…

# Introduction

Our dog Poppy on the lookout in Shouldham Warren in 2019…

Boats at high tide at Wells Next the Sea

Norfolk is on the east coast of England in the UK. In Norfolk, the coast road extends from the Wash at Kings Lynn down to Lowestoft and then inland as far as Thetford and then back to Kings Lynn. The capital city of Norfolk is Norwich which is also where I was born. We have no motorways in our county and only a few roads that have more than a single carriageway. This has helped Norfolk to maintain it's away from it all feel but also means that the narrow Norfolk roads can get somewhat congested in the height of the summer although this gives the many road travellers the time to take in the beautiful Norfolk countryside and coast. As part of this introduction we will now go back in time and meet two of my favourite all time Norfolk hero's…

# Introduction

# Queen Boudica of the Iceni tribe

Queen Boudica was a local Norfolk chieftain Queen who fought and almost defeated the mighty Roman Army, way back in the first century A.D. Her tribe the Iceni lived in what we now call Norfolk which is also the place of my birth, so like Lord Nelson, another Norfolk hero, I am very proud that Boudica was a local girl (actually she was born in Wales and came to Norfolk as a young bride). The village, where Susie and I live today, called Shouldham was in existence right back in the Roman and Iceni tribe era. Artifacts (Iceni and Roman coins) have recently been found in our village and these could have meant that Boudica could have even walked where we walk today. This really could be true and it excites my imagination!. Boudica was married to King Prasutagus and upon his death she was flogged by the Romans who she then went on to fight until her death in AD 61. In my painting above, I have tried to endow her with a sense of how I think she would have looked. She is reputed to have had red hair and wore a blue dye called woad on her face to make her more frightening to her enemies. Boudica is another great example of the important role females have played all through history and how with determination, pride and other warrior traits, even a gentle woman can make a very fearsome opponent…

# Introduction

# Horatio Nelson

Born on 29 September 1758 in Burnham Thorpe, Norfolk, Horatio Nelson was the sixth of the 11 children of a clergyman. He joined the navy aged 12, on a ship commanded by a maternal uncle. He became a captain at 20, and saw service in the West Indies, Baltic and Canada. When I was a teenager I use to stay with my Uncle Frank, Aunty Joyce and their daughter Beryl at North Creake during the summer holidays. I would often cycle to Burnham Market which is less than two miles away to walk in the footsteps of my Norfolk hero Nelson. You can still visit today the place of his birth and/or call into the local pub that bears his name (see above). The pub was actually Nelson's local and we now he drank there between 1787 to 1793 because in 1793, it's recorded that he threw a huge dinner party for the men of the village to celebrate his new command of H.M.S Agamemnon. He married Frances Nisbet in 1787 in Nevis, and returned to England with his bride to spend the next five years on half-pay, frustrated at the lack of a command. Nelson once said *"I am a Norfolk man and glory in being so"*. When Britain entered the French Revolutionary Wars in 1793, Nelson was given command of the Agamemnon. It was during the battle at Calvi that he lost the sight in his right eye). At the Battle of the Nile in 1798, he successfully destroyed Napoleon's fleet and thus his bid for a direct trade route to India. Nelson's next posting took him to Naples, where he fell in love with Emma, Lady Hamilton. Although they remained in their respective marriages, Nelson and Emma Hamilton considered each other soul-mates and had a child together, Horatia, in 1801. In that same year, Nelson was promoted to vice-admiral. From 1794 to 1805, under Nelson's leadership, the Royal Navy proved its supremacy over the French. His most famous engagement, at Cape Trafalgar, saved Britain from threat of invasion by Napoleon, but it would be his last. On the 21st October 1805, Nelson sent out the now famous signal to his fleet: **'England expects that every man will do his duty'**. He was killed by a French sniper a few hours later while leading the attack on the combined French and Spanish fleet. His body was preserved in a brandy barrel and transported back to England where he was given a state funeral. Now after our trip back in time we will now come right up to date by visiting the Norfolk coast and Wells Next the Sea…

# Introduction

Alan, Ginny, Gerard, Lou and Olivia on the beach and on the train
at Wells Next the Sea

One of Susie and my favourite places to spend a day in is Wells Next The Sea as it offers the visitor sandy beaches, a bustling harbour area, very good shopping and food opportunities. There is even a light narrow gauge railway that transports visitors from the beach to the harbour side and back again. We have visited this resort regularly from when I was a small child, through my teenage years, as a parent with Susie and Ginny and we continue to do so. It is, for us, an ideal place to unwind and relax in…

# Introduction

Alan resting on the hut steps, children on the beach and building a sand castle

The beach huts that stretch for quite a distance along Wells Next the Sea beach are not just a great place to relax in, get changed in, make a cup of tea in but to also shelter in from the occasional poor weather but they are also great to just sit in and watch the world go. As you can see from the picture above the steps of these beach huts also provide somewhere for the weary day tripper to rest for a while. For us and many others there is nothing like having a picnic on the beach, having a paddle in the sea before making sand castles. I have been coming to Wells Next the Sea since I was a very young boy and it is my and now Susie's all time favourite beach resort in Norfolk…

# Introduction

Ginny, Alan in days gone by and lets go fly a kite(s)

Some of Susie and my memories of our best days out were when Ginny was very young. On the days that we went out on a family day trip it was usually to the beach or into the Norfolk countryside to perhaps sit by a river, have a picnic, do some fishing, or even fly a kite. Sometimes we would even visit somewhere like Banham Zoo or any of the other brilliant visitor attractions that we have here in Norfolk. The thing about going out for a day by the seaside, in the countryside or visiting tourist attractions with younger children is that sometimes you have to provide a piggy back for those tired little legs!…

# Introduction

Wells Next the Sea is a favourite beach for one of our family fun days out

In more recent years we have often been accompanied on our visits to the Norfolk coast by our grown up daughter Ginny and/or Susie's sister Lou, husband Gerard and their daughter Olivia who live in Sheffield. I have always found that it is having the company of friends and/or family that helps to enhance our day trip enjoyment for us. By sharing these trips with others from further afield also increases my pride in the beautiful county of my birth Norfolk…

# Introduction

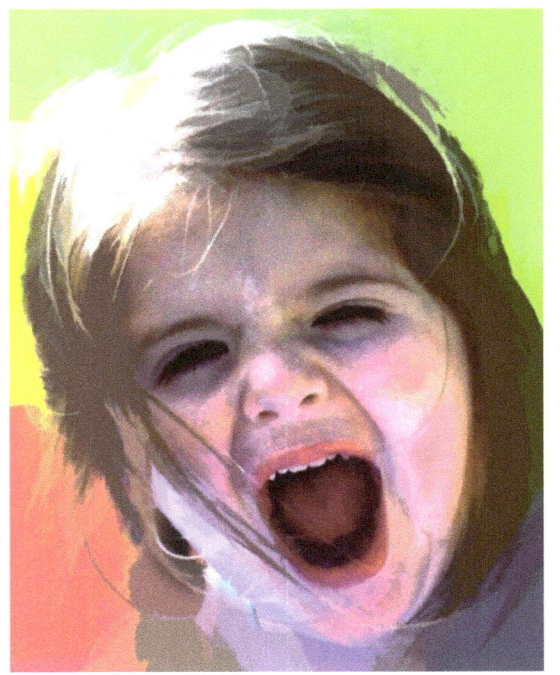

Olivia, Alan and our dogs Poppy and Charlie enjoying the sunshine
in the flatlands and the big skies of the County of Norfolk

It is very true that on warm sunny days there is nothing better than getting outside and exploring the Norfolk countryside. Wether it is walking, cycling or driving around in the countryside or even better going to the North Norfolk coast. You will always find great beauty and see plenty of people walking around with great big smiles on their faces. Welcome to Norfolk!…

# Introduction

The beautiful Norfolk wildlife and the pretty village of Litcham in Norfolk

Living in Norfolk as I do, with its great light and wide endless skies has inspired me to paint from a very early age. I think this wonderful light and space is demonstrated in my painting above of the village of Litcham and shows just how the light and space creates a kaleidoscope of many colours in my minds eye. So as the sun begins to set and the light begins to fade I will put my watercolour paints away, finish this introduction and now reflect on times gone by. In the next chapter, we will set off on our voyage of discover together by reading about some of the rich history of the beautiful county of Norfolk…

# The History of Norfolk

An old Norfolk boy and a map of Norfolk

Before looking at the Norfolk of today come with me as we learn something about it's past. Let us start at the very beginning of time where as we say in Norfolk lets go "a Mardling and a Troshin" in the old times of Norfolk. Norfolk is a rural county in the East of England in the UK. Knowledge of prehistoric Norfolk is limited by a lack of evidence although the earliest finds are from the end of the Lower Paleolithic period (2,500,000 to 300,000 BC). Communities have existed in Norfolk since the last Ice Age and tools, coins and other ancient hoards such as those found at Snettisham indicate the presence of an extensive and industrious population from very ancient times...

# The History of Norfolk

## The Lower Paleolithic (2,500,000 to 300,000 BC)

In 2005 it was discovered that Norfolk contained one of the earliest finds of the existence of "European Man". The find revealed flint tools, similar to those found on the Suffolk coast at Pakefield which were dated at around 668,000 BC and a find at Happisburgh in the "Cromer Forest Bed" has been dated as being 550,000 years old and has given us flints, bones and the oldest hand axe to be found in north-west Europe.

## The Middle Paleolithic (300,000 to 30,000 BC)

Stone Age flint tools

The age of man working with flint is significant in Norfolk as the county produced some of the best flint in the country for making stone age tools mainly from flint found at a site near Thetford. We know far more today about our stone age past than ever before thanks to local archaeologists and popular TV programmes such as Time Team. Flint tools produced from Norfolk flint have been excavated from not only all over the British Isle but in many countries overseas...

# The History of Norfolk

## The Middle Paleolithic (300,000 to 30,000 BC)

In 2002 there was a major discovery of one of the most important sites of Neanderthal man, dated to around 58,000 BC, in the Thetford Forest at Lynford. The site was found to contain organic material and a Mousterian hand axe was found in a good state of preservation. A further 30 Mousterian hand axes were found along with reindeer bones covered in cut marks. The animal remains have revealed the presence of woolly mammoths (see below), woolly rhinoceros, brown bears, spotted hyenas and other smaller remains such as fish jaws, frog bones and several types of mollusk Although the site contains such exotic animals the temperatures were still below those felt today as Norfolk was still in the clutches of the remnants of an Ice-Age.

## The Neolithic and Chalcolithic (9500 to 3000 BC)

Grimes Graves is the name given to a large and well-preserved group of Neolithic flint mines at a site near Brandon, Norfolk close to Thetford consisting of 400 pits. It was first named Grim's Graves by the Anglo-Saxons and was first excavated in 1870 when the pits were first identified as mines dug over 5,000 years ago. The average temperature in July has been estimated as 13°C and the area would have been below freezing for most of the winter months. From plant and insect remains it has been deduced that the area was marshy and covered with small areas of open still water similar to the modern day Norfolk Broads…

# The History of Norfolk

## The Neolithic and Chalcolithic (9500 to 3000 BC)

This period covers the stages of change from the pottery of the stone age into the age of metals. The Chalcolithic Age is the start of the Copper Age and marks the end of the time when people could only work mainly single element metals such as silver, tin, copper and gold. The Copper Age precedes the Bronze Age when metallurgy developed into a science capable of amalgamating metals into bronze and other compounds.

## The Bronze Age (3000 to 600 BC)

Norfolk was a centre of metalworking and by the Late Bronze Age northern Norfolk had developed into a major area of production. There were also throwbacks to the earlier ages and one such throwback was the monuments. A significant find was discovered in 1998 between the high and low tidal limits off the North West coast of Norfolk at Holme-next-the-Sea. A ring of timbers was found and within it was an upturned tree stump with its roots above the sand. The remains were excavated in 1999 and the samples taken dated it to 2049 BC. The monument got called Seahenge and is now on permanent display in the Kings Lynn Museum. A find at Sutton (near Stalham) on 7 July 1875 revealed a copper alloy shield buried under peat lying on, and covered by, white sand. There have been numerous finds from all periods of the Bronze Age but amongst the most notable were a find of 141 axes heads at Foulsham and pottery including collared urns from the Witton Wood barrow...

# The History of Norfolk

## The Iron Age

There is evidence that much of Norfolk was intensively farmed by people during the Late Iron Age. The Cenimagni tribe who submitted to Caesar in 54 BC had settled in both lowland and upland Norfolk by this time.

The Iceni tribe were centred in north-west Norfolk, where hordes of their coins and gold torcs have been discovered such as those found at Snettisham. Coins found in the south of the county indicate that the Iceni tribe (led by Queen Boudica already mentioned earlier) may have been centred around Thetford by the mid-1st century AD. The fields of Norfolk where these treasures have been found are now awash with poppies in the summer barley but who knows how many riches may still lay un-discovered under them...

# The History of Norfolk

## Roman Norfolk

Norfolk's coastline is markedly different today from the coastline that existed when the Romans first occupied what is now the county of Norfolk. The northern coast of Norfolk has eroded over the last two millennia, parts of it perhaps having retreated by up to 2 kilometres (1.2 miles). The eastern coast was dominated by an enormous estuary, the island of Flegg and a peninsular (modern Lothingland). The Wash was much larger in size and the area now known as the Fens was impenetrable marsh containing isolated islands surrounded by water. The River Waveney between Norfolk and Suffolk was at that time a substantial feature. After the Romans conquered Britain in 43 AD, forts, villas, towns and roads were constructed around Norfolk as the Roman army became established. Major Roman roads in the county included the Peddars Way and Pye Road. After a minor rebellion by the Iceni in 47 AD King Prasutagus was allowed to rule independently as a client king. On his death in 60 AD Roman rule was imposed on the territory and his widow Boudica was not allowed to succeed him as Roman law only allowed male heirs to claim a client king's title. After Boudica was humiliated and her daughters raped she led a rebellion in which the towns of Colchester (Camulodunum), London (Londinium) and St. Albans (Verulamium) were sacked.

Boudica's (seen above) rebellion in 60 AD, caused by the imposition of direct rule by the Romans, was followed by order and peace, which lasted until the Roman armies left Britain in about 410 AD...

# The History of Norfolk

## Roman Norfolk

Following the defeat of Boudica the Romans restored order on the region by establishing an administrative Centre at *Venta Icenorum* (the present day Caistor St. Edmund), a small town built at Brampton and other settlements which were developed at river crossings or road junctions. The mostly rural population lived in scattered homesteads, villages or more affluent Roman villas. The level of the sea fell during Roman times and the swamps in the west of Norfolk slowly dried out. The land was then able to be converted into fertile farmland where sheep-rearing and salt production could be established. The Saxon Shore forts were built by the Romans in the 3rd century AD as a defence against overseas raiders. When you look around Norfolk the ruins of the forts built at Burgh Castle (Roman Gariannonum), guarding the estuary across from the island of Flegg, still exist, but there is now little remaining of the forts at Brancaster (Branodunum) built on the north coast, and at Caister-on-Sea, on the east coast and near Burgh Castle.

After the last of the armies of Rome had left our shores in 410 AD most of the visible remains of Roman Britain slowly disappeared over time...

# The History of Norfolk

## Anglo-Saxon Norfolk

After 410 AD, tribes arrived from north-west Europe and intermingled with the Romano-Britons already living in the Norfolk region. The new culture of the Anglo-Saxons replaced the culture of the Romans and ancient Britons (so that for instance there are now few place-names in Norfolk that pre-date the Anglo-Saxon period). The first written record of most of the place names in the county is the 11th-century Domesday Book, but these names will have existed much earlier. Places with names ending in -ham in Norfolk (but not those ending -ingham) are generally sited favourably by rivers or near fertile soil and grew in importance from large villages into the county's modern market towns. Less important settlements tended to end with the suffixes -ton, -wick or -stead. Swaffham in Norfolk has Anglo-Saxon origins.

Swaffham Town

Excavations and place-name evidence indicates that the early Anglo-Saxons (pre-800 AD) seem to have occupied the south and south-west of Norfolk most densely, with settlements concentrated along river systems. A settlement and a cemetery at Spong Hill, containing both graves and inhumation pots, is an example of one of the few early Saxon sites to have been found in Norfolk. During the 7th century East Anglia adopted Christianity and the custom of burying grave goods, found at numerous burial sites, eventually ceased…

# The History of Norfolk

## Anglo-Saxon Norfolk

Helmet of an Anglo-Saxon King

As we have seen the arrival of the Anglo-Saxons caused the loss of much Roman and British culture in Norfolk. It is known from external evidence from excavations and place-names that by c. 800 AD all Norfolk had been settled and the first towns had emerged. Norfolk was the northern half of the Kingdom of East Anglia and was ruled by the Anglo-Saxon Wuffing dynasty. The Saxons eventually settled evenly over the uplands and lowlands of Norfolk. By 850 AD the majority of the county's current pre-Danish place names had been created. Evidence of the importance of the emerging trade settlements of Thetford and Norwich is still being discovered. Numerous other sites in the county have revealed evidence of Saxon settlement, for instance at North Elmham(where there is evidence of timber buildings and roadways), or at Bawsey (with finds of pottery, coins and metalwork). Six late Anglo-Saxon silver brooches were discovered at Pentney in 1978, which may have belonged to a local maker or dealer. Norfolk was part of the Kingdom of the East Angles during much of the Anglo-Saxon period. Its history is largely obscure: much information is based on mediaeval chronicles and often cannot be verified. The history of Norfolk, the northern half of the Kingdom, cannot be distinguished from the rest of East Anglia during this period...

# The History of Norfolk

## The Vikings in Norfolk

The only surviving lists of the Kings of East Anglia are those written by mediaeval sources, such as William of Malmesbury. Nothing is known about any of the Kings from 664 to 747 AD, after which the succession and genealogy of the Kings of East Anglia after this time is uncertain.

Eric the Viking…

The Vikings attacked Norfolk in 865 AD and four years later killed Edmund, the last king of the East Angles. Villages on the former island of Flegg with names such as Scratby, Hemsby and Filby provide evidence of Viking settlement with other place-names of Viking origin scattered around Norfolk. Viking settlement is thought to have stimulated the growth of towns such as Norwich and Thetford. After Edward the Elder conquered East Anglia and ended Viking domination in 917 AD, the region was absorbed into the Kingdom of England…

# The History of Norfolk
## Mediaeval Norwich

At the time of the Norman Conquest, Norfolk formed part of the earldom of Harold I of England and offered no active resistance to William the Conqueror, who bestowed the earldom of East Anglia on Ralph de Gael. Under the Normans, the City of Norwich emerged as the hub of the region. With steady growth and strong overseas links it became an important mediaeval city, but it suffered from internal tensions, un sanitary conditions and disastrous fires. Mediaeval Norfolk was the mostly densely populated and the most productive agricultural region in the country. Land was cultivated intensively and the wool trade was sustained by huge flocks. Other industries such as peat extraction were important. Norfolk was a prosperous county and possessed a wealth of monastic establishments and parish churches. After the Revolt of the Earls in 1075 AD, Earl Ralph's estates were forfeited and passed to Roger Bigod. Norwich Cathedral is one of the great Norman buildings of England. The arrival of the Normans in 1066 AD led to the destruction of much of Anglo-Saxon Norwich. After Ralph de Gael rebelled against the King, a large part of the town was burned by the Normans in retribution. They then started to develop Norwich into a prosperous international port and a centre of Norman power.

Norwich Castle…

Norwich Castle was built by 1075. It was of a motte and bailey type and was rebuilt in stone before 1200 AD. Work on the cathedral precinct started in 1096 AD. Within it was built a cathedral church, a fortified bishop's palace and other monastic buildings. The formation of the precinct turned a large part of the town into an unpopulated area of quarry pits and building yards. Early mediaeval Norwich grew into a cosmopolitan city and expanded around the waterfront and westwards along St. Benedict's Street…

# The History of Norfolk

## Mediaeval Norwich

Norwich...

During the 12th century there was a thriving Jewish community in Norwich, but it was unpopular with the Christian population. In 1144 AD the Jews were accused of the ritual murder of a young boy named William, who was subsequently canonized. Their synagogue was destroyed in 1286 AD and four years later all the Jews in England were expelled from the country. Tensions between the cathedral priory and the citizens of Norwich (in part over the jurisdiction of land in the city) culminated in the Riot of 1272 AD, in which thirteen members of the priory were murdered and the precinct gates and St. Ethelbert's Church were destroyed. As punishment, the main anarchists were put to death and the city lost its liberties and was forced to pay for the building of a new gate for the priory. Between 1297 AD and 1344 AD a new defensive wall was constructed on the huge banks that surrounded the city, these were done to replace the earlier palisade and gates. The area enclosed was the largest for any city in England, although inside was a considerable amount of pasture land, which was slowly absorbed as new monastic settlements, houses, markets and industrial sites, appeared. In 1348-1350 AD the Black Death may have killed two fifths of the population of the city. It led to efforts to improve the sanitary conditions, but these had little impact. Immigration from the surrounding countryside soon restored pre-plague numbers, partly as a result of the growing textiles industry. By 1400 AD Norwich had grown to become a major city of perhaps 10,000 inhabitants. Growing civic wealth and pride was reflected in new large buildings such as the Guildhall, built from 1407 AD to 1453 AD. During the later mediaeval period, Norwich's fortunes declined. Both the fires of 1412 AD and 1413 AD (which destroyed many of the city's buildings) and the Wars of the Roses, contributed to its decline. The period is characterised by a growing gap between the wealthy and the poor people of Norwich...

# The History of Norfolk

## Mediaeval Norfolk

In the 14th century Norfolk was the most densely populated and most intensively farmed region in England. The land was predominantly arable, much more so than in previous centuries. Where land could not be ploughed easily, it was managed as pasture.

The woodlands of much of Norfolk were cleared during mediaeval times. The soils of the county were variously light, heavy and – most valuably – moderate. The moderately heavy soils were concentrated in central and eastern parts. Crops that were grown included barley (for the making of beer), rye, oats and peas. Horses were introduced sooner in Norfolk than elsewhere and crop rotation helped to intensify cultivation. Manorial records show that the types of crops cultivated and animals stocked depended on access to markets, labour supply, freedom from communal controls and transport costs, as well as soil type. In comparison to its arable land, Norfolk's pastures and meadows were less productive. In the 12$^{th}$ century an Augustinian Abbey was built at North Creake and a keep at Castle Rising. As with the rest of the country, the Church was central to mediaeval life in Norfolk. Far more mediaeval parish churches were built than in any other county in England. Norwich alone once had sixty-two churches. Over time the numbers have slowly declined, due to depopulation, competition or local re-organisation. Many new monastic communities were established in Norfolk during the Middle Ages…

# The History of Norfolk
# The Norfolk Broads

The Norfolk Broads owe there existence to the large-scale extraction of peat and clay during the Middle Ages. They were once deep pits, up to 15 feet (4.6 m) in depth, from which an enormous amount of peat was dug over a period of centuries. Peat extraction may have begun during the Anglo-Saxon period, but the first evidence of the industry in Norfolk is from mediaeval abbey records. John of Oxnead is the first chronicler to record the major floods that recurred during this period, as the sea breached the vulnerable east coast and devastated the land. As a result of flooding, the extraction of peat declined and the records change from peat-digging accounts to descriptions of fen, marsh, fisheries and the importing of sea-coal from the north-east of England. Over a long period the battle to obtain peat and clay from the pits was steadily lost, as they become water-logged and then permanently flooded and all memory of the origin of the new 'Broads' was lost. In the wars between King John and his barons Roger Bigod garrisoned Norwich Castle against the King, who in 1216 AD on his retreat from Lynn lost his baggage in The Wash. Norfolk returned members to parliament in 1290 AD, and in 1298 AD the county and the boroughs of Kings Lynn, Norwich and Great Yarmouth returned each two members. The story of Julian of Norwich (1342 – 1429) also dates to this period. She is noted as being the first woman to have written a book in English so by me being a Norfolk artist, writer and author I am following a long line of Norfolk writers...

# The History of Norfolk

## Norfolk legends

One of the legends from Norfolk dating to the 14th century is that of the Pedlar of Swaffham. The legacy of this tale can be seen to this day on the market place town signpost and in the choir area of the parish church. Here stand two wooden pews. One has the carvings of a pedlar and his dog, the other of a woman looking over the door of a shop...

# The History of Norfolk

## Norfolk during the Tudors and the Stuarts

## Kett's Rebellion in Norfolk

After the enclosures of local landowners around Norfolk were destroyed, thousands of people joined Robert Kett in a march on Norwich, forming a large organised camp on Mousehold Heath that overlooks the City. After a failed attempt by the authorities to disperse them on the offer of a general pardon, Norwich's city gates were shut to the rebels, who nevertheless managed to breach the defences and occupy the city. In London, the government responded to the crisis by sending the Marquis of Northampton to regain Norwich, who initially entered the city unopposed, but was forced by the rebels to withdraw with his army to Cambridge. From this point, Kett was less successful. He failed in an attempt to spread the rebellion to Great Yarmouth. The Earl of Warwick reached Norwich and gained entry to the city with a large force. Although outnumbered, Kett's men rejected an offer of a free pardon and after bloody street fighting they were forced to return to Mousehold Heath. Kett made an attempt to recapture the city, but the arrival of mercenaries in support of Warwick forced him to abandon the camp. In a bloody pitched battle outside the city, the rebels were routed and Kett was captured...

# The History of Norfolk

## Norfolk during the English Civil War

The county supported Parliament during the English Civil War, although there was a strong element of Royalist support. The defences of Norwich and the main ports were strengthened and in December 1642 AD the Eastern Association was formed to place the region on a war footing, but little blood was shed in Norfolk, which was held by Parliament throughout the war. In September 1643 AD, an anti-Papist mob caused considerable damage to Norwich Cathedral, which was occupied by troops the following year. The only serious fighting in Norfolk during the civil war was at King's Lynn, where Royalist sympathies were strongest. In April 1643 Parliament investigated King's Lynn and ordered the detention of the town's prominent Royalists. That August, on the assurance that Royalist forces would soon arrive, the town declared openly for the King. It was besieged by the Earl of Manchester and suffered damage from bombardment, but Parliament's attempts to raise sufficient forces was beset by difficulties and the town surrendered only after Manchester declared that on 16 September he would storm the defences. Any Royalist hopes of assisting the King in Norfolk was at an end…

# The History of Norfolk

# The 17th Century in Norfolk

Rabbits were the food for many of the people of Norfolk in this period

In 1646 AD a series of events started that would lead to one of the Norfolk's most noteworthy disasters. Tension had been growing in the county due to rising taxation in the face of rising grain prices, coupled with increasing amounts of interference by the central government in county affairs. This led to numerous acts of resistance across the county in 1646 AD, including rioting in Norwich and King's Lynn. The county's largest city, Norwich, was divided between supporters of the traditional culture and Puritans. In 1647 AD the city's citizens elected John Utting, an act that angered local Puritans, who managed to obtain orders for him to be detained in London. When a Parliamentary representative attempted to arrest Utting, the situation became literally explosive. On 24 April 1648 AD angry townsfolk in Norwich rioted and attacked the homes of prominent Puritans. A small contingent of Parliamentary troops arrived and managed to gain entry into the city, leading to running battles along St. Stephens street. During this confused period, rioters who had taken possession of the armory contained in the Royalist Committee House on Bethel Street accidentally ignited the barrels of black powder stored there, leading to a tremendous explosion causing immense destruction to the city and great loss of life. This explosion came to be known as "The Great Blow," bringing the rioting in the city to an abrupt end!...

# The History of Norfolk

## 18th Century Norfolk

1785 AD and 1786 AD saw the first Aviation Activity in the county of Norfolk when several manned gas balloon flights were made from Quantrell's Gardens in Norwich.

It was time for School

## 19th Century Norfolk

In the middle of the nineteenth century, over a hundred Norfolk families owned estates greater than 2,000 acres (8.1 km²; 3.1 sq mi) in size, and there were numerous smaller landowners in the county. After 1875 AD, a long depression in English agriculture and industry set in, which reduced estate incomes and put severe pressure on their owners, a situation made worse by the accumulation of debts due to family settlements or extravagant expenditure, often sustained over generations, and the introduction of Death Duties in 1894 AD. Indebted landowners were forced to sell their possessions, let their estates for shooting, reduce staff levels or take up residence elsewhere. Estates became neglected as their owners strived to save money and many estates disappeared as farms, parks and woodland were sold off and halls were left to decay. After 1880 AD many larger estates changed hands, were broken up or reduced in size as land was acquired by farmers and businessmen from outside the county. A housing boom during the 1890's driven by a dramatic increase in Norfolk's population enabled some landowners on the outskirts of towns and coastal resorts to profit from the sale of their land...

# The History of Norfolk

## 20th Century Norfolk

The First World War was significant to the county of Norfolk in a number of ways. Large numbers of men of fighting age were called up to join local regiments that were sent to fight in France; virtually every Norfolk village has a war memorial that records the names of those who lost their lives. The war was the first time that significant aviation activity spread throughout the county with a large number of aerodromes and landing grounds being built. Significantly Pulham Market in the south of the county was one of the few locations where airships were stationed. Boulton and Paul in Norwich and Savages of Kings Lynn were both involved in aircraft production each company producing many hundreds of aircraft for the war effort and remained in aviation as late as the 1960's. As well as Boulton and Paul, the firm of Lawrence Scott & Electromotors was also involved in the war effort, providing shells as well as electrical motors and other components for the Navy. The county was one of the first places on earth bombed from the air when German Zeppelin airships raided the county a number of times. Late in the war Zeppelin L 70 was shot down off the Norfolk Coast and all on board were killed, a number of the men being buried in churchyards along the coast. The Second World War brought similar sacrifices, damage and suffering as the First World War had done to the people of Norfolk. In more recent times Norfolk has continued its farming traditions with tourism now playing an important part in the local economy.

## Norwich City - We are the Champions my Friend!

Norwich City FC players, manager, staff and supporters were celebrating promotion back to the premier league in 2015 and again this May 2019. I am proud to say that I have been a fan for over sixty years. I hope there is much more success for my team in the years that lay ahead.

Today in Norfolk you will still see fields of wheat, corn, poppies and lavender with the addition of clusters of modern day wind turbines. Having now completed a tour through the history of Norfolk we will begin our journey into the Norfolk of today and the county of my birth by enjoying the famous, beautiful and spectacular Coast of Norfolk...

# The Norfolk Coast

The Norfolk coast is one of the treasures of the county with golden sandy beaches, lovely sand dunes, active seascapes, diverse wildlife and enormous skies. Starting on the west coast at Kings Lynn the coast road passes through many of the best resort towns and villages this county has to offer. As we travel along the coast road in a clockwise direction from west to east some of the places that we would visit are:

Kings Lynn, Hunstanton, Old Hunstanton, Holkham, Wells, Blakeney, Cley, Sheringham, Cromer, Walcott, Sea Palling, Mundesley, Hemby, Caister, Great Yarmouth, Gorleston before finally finishing up at the resort of Lowestoft.

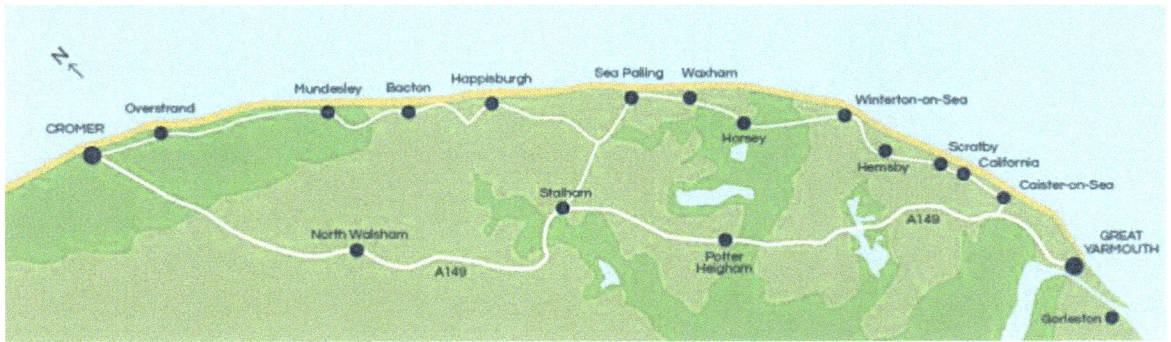

Map of a section of the Norfolk coast and boats waiting for the tide to turn

# The Norfolk Coast

Beach huts on Wells Next the Sea beach

Holidaymakers looking at the boats in Wells Next the Sea harbour

# The Norfolk Coast

## Wells Next the Sea

Wells Next the Sea harbour and maltings

The harbour at Wells Next the Sea was the most important gateway for the early shipping of barley from Norfolk. In the past there were hundreds of maltings in the town and half the countries malt was exported from here. The town once had two railway lines which it was thought would promote Wells Next the Sea as an import and export port and push the maltings to a whole new level. But today there is barely a glimmer if industry or export trade happening in the town. As the silt in the harbour grew deeper it became harder and harder for bigger boats to trade from its port and Wells struggled to live up to its billing of a "major port". Today the town is in something of a time warp however, with its quay side now a favourite spot for children trying to catch small crabs. Its narrow streets leading uphill from the harbour side has numerous gift shops and fast food outlets. There is a small gauge model railway that carries visitors from the harbour down to the dunes and its long sandy beach. Wells Next the Sea is just the place that appeals to its 21$^{st}$ century visitors! Susie and I love it…

# The Norfolk Coast

Wells Next the Sea beach huts, a fox and a kingfisher

Alan, Ginny, Olivia, Lou and Gerard on the beach at Wells Next the Sea

# The Norfolk Coast

Catch of the day

Gerard, Lou and Olivia all aboard the Wells Next the Sea narrow gauge railway

# The Norfolk Coast

## Brancaster Staithe

Further along the coast from Wells Next the Sea is the Brancaster Malthouse which was once the best example of the industrialisation of Norfolk's agriculture. It was completed in 1797 and was 100 metres long and processed 120 tons of barley grain every week. Norfolk barley was used amongst other uses for making whiskey in Scotland, beer in Holland and Guinness in Dublin. Today nothing remains of the maltings and Brancaster Staithe is now a sleepy Norfolk village much loved by visitors for its scenic beauty.

The beach, the quay and boats at Brancaster Staithe

# The Norfolk Coast

Ship wreck on the beach and walking on the promenade at Sheringham

Norfolk beach huts

# The Norfolk Coast

## Sheringham

The Sheringham high street, an owl and a long tailed tit

The seaside town of Sheringham is the home of the North Norfolk Railway and has been enthralling steam enthusiasts for nearly 50 years. The town itself is compact with a high street running down from the railway station to the sea front and there are plenty of shopping opportunities along the way. In the past, mainline trains arrived at Cromer from 1887 onwards. The tourism industry was just beginning in the late Victorian times and all the new railway lines along the North Norfolk coast were aimed at being used by the holidaymaker. This venture was successful and the profits made during the summer season kept the trains running during the winter. Sheringham became a victim of the severe reduction in the provision of railway line destinations in the 1960's when the railway mainline was closed and the resort suffered greatly as a result. In more recent times Sheringham has become a favoured place to retire too and with the advent of the family car and people having more leisure time the town has seen an increase in visitor numbers in recent years…

# The Norfolk Coast

Rough seas and the north beach at Mundesley

Members of our family enjoying the Norfolk coast

# The Norfolk Coast

Kings Lynn and boat on a Norfolk beach

Alan on a Norfolk beach, Cromer pier, fox cub and going in for the kill

# The Norfolk Coast

## Hunstanton

The cliffs, Ginny riding and Susie waiting on Hunstanton beach

Known to the locals as "Sunny Hunny" Hunstanton is on the North West tip of Norfolk. The railways came to Hunstanton in 1862 and this led to more and more people wanting to come and sample the bracing sea air and swim in the sea! The railway line also passed close to Sandringham House that is the Norfolk home of our Royal Family. This added to the attraction of travelling from the Midlands and London to holiday in this somewhat remote spot in England. At that time sea water was heralded as a wonder drug. Swimming in it could cure everything, it was claimed, so the upper class flocked to seaside resorts such as Brighton, Weymouth, Eastbourne and to a lesser extent to Sunny Hunny. Because of this Hunstanton grew and grew until the dreaded mainline railway closures of the 60's but ever resilient Sunny Hunny today is still a very popular holidaymaker destination with its donkey rides on the sandy beach, the sea life centre and its many gift shopping opportunities. The resort now caters mainly for family fun packed days out…

# The Norfolk Coast

# The Holkham Estate

Situated on the North Norfolk coast is the Holkham Estate which was owned by the ultimate Norfolk farmer, Thomas William Coke. Of all the great Norfolk estates Holkham is the largest of around 30,000 acres. Queen Victory visited the estate and made the aging Coke, Earl of Leicester. His lands stretched from the coast well inland and the park he created stands at around 3000 acres alone. In honour of the Queens visit the new Earl of Leicester built a pub on the edge of his park, in honour of his Queen called "The Victoria". Visitors to the county can still have a good meal and/or a drink in this pub today which overlooks the dunes, beach and the North Sea.

Queen Victoria and the dunes and the sea at Holkam

# The Norfolk Coast

## Great Yarmouth

Great Yarmouth is the most built up resort on the Norfolk coast and has long been popular with summer holidaymaker's from the industrial heartland of Great Britain.

## Hemsby

Hemsby is also a great place to visit and with its golden sandy beach and dunes it is a favourite with the holidaymakers of Norfolk and beyond.

Susie relaxing on a beach in Norfolk

# The Norfolk Coast

Cromer pier in the sunshine and boats and purple sky in Norfolk

Members of our family out and about in Norfolk

# The Norfolk Coast

## Cromer

Alan wandering around in Cromer

Norfolk Poppies…

The seaside town of Cromer is a trully Victorian holiday invention. The arcitecture of this Norfolk gem reflects this era. Cromer was marketed as "Poppyland" in its heyday and anyone who was anyone in the 1890's came here. The name Poppyland was coined to reflect all of the fields of barley that had red poppies growing through it that the train passengers would see when steaming through the Norfolk countryside. In 1901 Cromer pier was opened to create an eye-catching centre-piece and a place of visitor entertainment. Today Cromer remains on the mainline railway unlike many of it's fellow Norfolk resorts and is still a popular place for holiday makers and day trippers alike…

# The Norfolk Coast

Boats at Burnham Overy and the beach at Sea Palling

Norfolk wildlife

# The Norfolk Coast

The Norfolk coastal resort of Blakeney

Lady in a Norfolk lavender field, a hare and some beach huts

# The Norfolk Coast

## Blakeney

Blakeney harbour

Boats and a seal at Blakeney…

Much of the land around the coastal resort of Blakeney is owned by the National Trust which has ensured that the wildlife and the beauty of this Norfolk gem has remained un-altered over many years. Blakeney was the first coastal nature reserve in the country and has done much to promote the conservation of it's seals, wildfowl and help ensure that this coastline would never get developed. Today Blakeney is a favourite haunt of the sailing fraternity and holidaymaker's alike who enjoy it's fine hotel, pubs, scenic views and it's bracing sea air…

# The Norfolk Coast

The beach at Bacton and through the gate and onto the beach at Bacton

Landscapes of Norfolk

# The Norfolk Coast

Norfolk wildlife and the coast

# The Norfolk Coast

Susie and Olivia on the beach and the cliffs at Hunstanton

Gorleston by the Sea, Cromer beach and collecting a boat of Cromer beach

# The Norfolk Coast

Alan sitting on the beach hut steps at Wells Next the Sea
enjoying the beach with its wonderful sea view, its big open skies,
its multitude of beautiful wildlife nearby and the golden soft sand
That is just waiting for you to build your sand castles on!

As we finish our journey around the fabulous coast of Norfolk I hope you will agree with me that we are very lucky to have so much beauty to be proud of in the county of my birth. In the more than seventy years that I have lived in this county I have visited all of the places featured in this book both during family holiday's staying in caravans and cabins beside the sea or on day trips into the countryside and coast and even during the course of my work. I have been so very lucky to have been born, raised and to have lived in this wonderful county and experience all that Norfolk has to offer. I am very proud to be a old Norfolk boy! In the next chapter we will go out and about to see what else Norfolk has to offer the visitor and see more of the sights that await them. …

# Out and About in Norfolk

In Norfolk we have no motorways and very little duel carriageways so the narrow roads of Norfolk can get quite congested in the spring and summer months. There are trains into Norwich and Kings Lynn from major UK cities but only a few local train lines exist that can take the visitor to other places within Norfolk. The trains go to Great Yarmouth, Lowestoft, Cromer and a few other places along the way. Buses run from Kings Lynn and Norwich bus stations throughout most of Norfolk but they are often infrequent at best. The best way to see Norfolk today is by using your own transport be it car, cycle or some other motorised transport or in some cases even walking!

Wells Next the Sea harbour and children and adults fishing for crabs

The narrow gauge train that runs between the beach and the harbour

# Out and About in Norfolk

The family with their buckets and spades on Wells Next the Sea beach

An owl and Ginny enjoying a day out by the river at Fakenham

# Out and About in Norfolk

A day out at Thrigby Hall is great fun and they have all sorts of wild animals to see like Tigers

Shopping on the high street in Thetford

# Out and About in Norfolk

The village of North Creake

All steamed up at Sheringham station

# Out and About in Norfolk

Sandringham House home to our Royal Family

## Sandringham House

In 1862 the then Queen Victoria purchased Sandringham House and the surrounding estate, for the equivalent of £22 million in today's money. The house on the estate has continued to be a Royal Residence up to the present day and our current Queen Elizabeth II and her family stay here at Christmas time every year and join my fellow Norfolk folk in the local church to worship. Much of the grounds and even the house, on certain dates, are open to the public and Susie and I often go to the country shows and fairs held in the grounds of the house every year. You can still visit the Royal Station at Wolferton near Sandringham but the line has long gone as it was another victim of the line closures programme of the 1960's. The estate also offers great walks and with Dersingham Bog within easy walking distance you get the rare chance to see what Norfolk would have been like centuries ago. The bog is a rare example of lowland heath with its bed of acid peat that once formed the landscape of much of the lands close to the fens. Dersingham Bog is now a protected nature reserve and is home to insects galore, amongst them the rare black darter dragonfly…

# Out and About in Norfolk

Norwich Castle

A Norfolk Wherry and a Windmill

# Out and About in Norfolk

Norfolk field of red poppies

Sunset on the Norfolk coast

# Out and About in Norfolk

Lavender growing in a Norfolk field

Wheat growing in a Norfolk field

# Out and About in Norfolk

Bringing in the harvest

## Lowestoft

Holidaymakers like nothing better than to stroll along Lowestoft towns promenade. Many think that this is a great way to enjoy the bracing sea air. People have been coming to Lowestoft to do just that for many, many years. The train still runs to the town from Norwich and provides easy access to the town from far and wide. My Mum's family came from the town and her father was the captain of a fishing boat that sailed out from the town harbour in years gone by…

# Out and About in Norfolk

Kings Lynn

Waiting for the tapes to go up at Kings Lynn speedway

# Out and About in Norfolk

Norfolk Seahenge which is now on displayed at Kings Lynn museum

Norfolk fishing boat

# Out and About in Norfolk

Something you will not see today is the famous Kings Lynn skyline building "The Campbell's Tower". They made soup and it was demolished in 2015 to make way for a Tesco supermarket which we shop in every week

Wells Next The Sea harbour

# Out and About in Norfolk

Hunstanton's Sea Life Sanctuary

All the fun of the fair on the Hunstanton beach front

# Out and About in Norfolk

Shopping in Norwich City centre

Lavender growing in a Norfolk field

# Out and About in Norfolk

Walking in the lovely Norfolk village of Horning

Boats on Wells Next the Sea harbour quay

# Out and About in Norfolk

Great Yarmouth

Downham Market

# Out and About in Norfolk

Steam Train at Dereham station which is open to the public

Sunset at Sheringham

# Out and About in (Skiathos) Norfolk

In the next few pages, just for a change of pace, I would like to share with you a place that is not in Norfolk but is somewhere far, far away from the UK that Susie and I also love very much:

## The Greek island of Skiathos

Pictures of the Greek island of Skiathos

# Out and About in (Skiathos) Norfolk

### TROULOS BAY HOTEL – SKIATHOS

### TROULOS BAY HOTEL – SKIATHOS

FROM THE HOTEL ONTO TROULOS BAY BEACH

Pictures of the Greek island of Skiathos

# Out and About in (Skiathos) Norfolk

Pictures of the Greek island of Skiathos

# Out and About in (Skiathos) Norfolk

WE LOVE SKIATHOS......

Picture of the Greek island of Skiathos

After enjoying a happy summer holiday on Skiathos it is always nice to get back home to my beloved Norfolk. We will therefore, now resume our journey once more by going out and about in Norfolk…

# Out and About (back) in Norfolk

Lightning strikes a Norfolk field

Snowy beach huts at Wells Next The Sea

# Out and About in Norfolk

Beach huts and members of our family at Wells Next the Sea

During my seventy plus years I have visited all of the places illustrated in this chapter firstly with my parents as a child, then with my own children on family day trips, also when working and in more recent years with my wife Susie. We have, as you have seen, also stepped outside of my beloved Norfolk for our summer holidays, from time to time, our favourite holiday destination is the paradise Greek Island of Skiathos. Now that we have been out and about in the Norfolk of today and paused for a while to visit Skiathos it is time, in the next chapter, to focus on times gone by and see the people, wildlife and places in Norfolk from years gone by. To do this I have used black and white pictures to try and convey a sense of a bygone era. So let's all buckle up and go back in time together!…

# Norfolk in Black and White

A misty Norfolk morning

The harbour at Blakeney

# Norfolk in Black and White

Thatching a Norfolk cottage

Delivering the beer

# Norfolk in Black and White

Riding on Holkham beach

Going down river to collect the reeds

# Norfolk in Black and White

A Norfolk windmill

Messing around in boats

# Norfolk in Black and White

Ploughing the land

Wherry's sailing on the Norfolk Broads

# Norfolk in Black and White

Fishermen mending their lobster pots at Sheringham

Fishing for eels in the Norfolk fens

# Norfolk in Black and White

Beach huts at Wells Next The Sea

A Norfolk windmill

# Norfolk in Black and White

There were lots of airfields located in Norfolk during World War Two and they all played a key and significant roll during the battle of Britain and later in wining the war! Above we see some of these brave men walking away from one of their squadron aircraft after returning safely from yet another sortie!

Norfolk farming folk.

As we take our leave of the brave men above and the hardworking farming folk it is time to go back into colour. In the next chapter we will be finding out more about some of the villages, towns and the City of Norwich that are all to be found in "My Norfolk"…

# My Norfolk

Norfolk is on the east coast of England. It has a spectacular coastline, with long sandy beaches, high cliffs, sand dunes, flint pebble banks and salt marshes. It is also well known for the Norfolk Broads, an extensive waterway network that can be fully explored by boat. In Norfolk there are many towns and villages, all with their own individual characters. The port of Kings Lynn has a long trading history, and today it still has large trade links with the rest of Europe. Norfolk is a firm favourite with families because of its traditional seaside resorts such as Great Yarmouth, Wells Next the Sea, Sheringham and Cromer, all with beautiful sandy beaches and great entertainment. Norfolk has many historic houses and museums and over 650 medieval churches, which is more than any other county in England. There are art galleries, country parks, steam railways and bird reserves aplenty and pedestrianised shopping centres in Norwich, Great Yarmouth and in Kings Lynn…

# My Norfolk

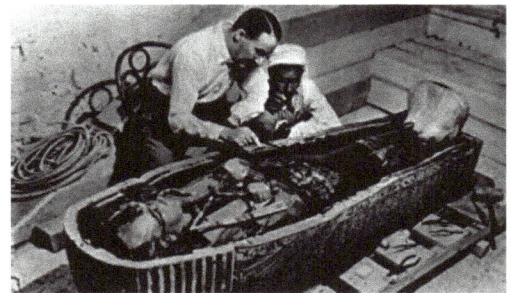
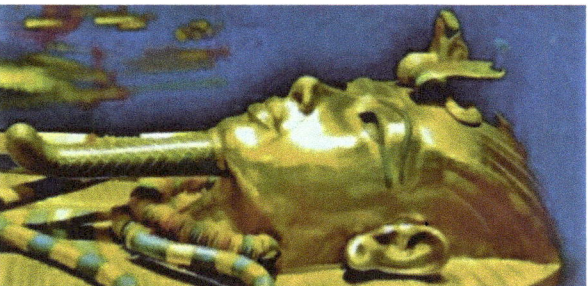

The county of Norfolk has a rich and varied history of invasion and conquest, but it was the Romans who came here and put their stamp on the county the most, much of which you can still see today in some beautiful and diverse locations. Famous people have called Norfolk their home. These include Queen Boudica of the Iceni tribe, Vice Admiral Horatio Nelson born in Burnham Thorpe and Howard Carter who found the Tomb of Tutankhamun in the Valley of the Kings in Egypt and lived for some time in the Town of Swaffham. The magnificent Roman Burgh Castle at Great Yarmouth and the Roman regional capital at Venta Icenorum at Caistor St Edmund near Norwich are all well worth a visit. Norfolk really has got something for everybody. If you are looking for somewhere to relax, or somewhere to explore, you will not be disappointed when you visit the beautiful county of Norfolk…

# My Norfolk

## The Norfolk Broads

Until the 1950's it was believed that the Norfolk Broads were just a feature of the natural landscape. Since then however the history of the Broads has been proved to be somewhat different. In the 1950's Dr Joyce Lambert examined the sides of the lakes and discovered them to be vertical rather than gently sloping as one might have expected. This suggested that rather than being naturally formed the Broads were in fact man made. Throughout the 12th century Norwich and Yarmouth were thriving and as a result the population in east Norfolk was growing rapidly. Monasteries began to excavate peat by hand and export it to the towns and cities as an alternative fuel source to timber, which was becoming scarce. Peat digging or 'turbary' soon became a thriving industry, it is believed that Norwich Cathedral took delivery of 320,000 tonnes of peat per year, and soon peat digging took place all across the eastern part of Norfolk…

# My Norfolk

In the 14th century, sea levels gradually rose and the peat pits began to fill up with water, flooding became more and more common until eventually the pits had to be abandoned. As a result over 125 miles of channels and Broads had been created and throughout the 16th century provided essential routes for trade, with Wherries transporting wool and agricultural produce from Norwich to Great Yarmouth for export by sea worldwide. The arrival of the railways in the 18th century meant less and less produce was being transported by river, and more and more people were beginning to travel to the area for their summer holidays. By the late 19th century a number of small businesses had set up offering yachts to hire. This was the beginning of boating holidays on the Norfolk Broads. The man-made Broads National Park is the third largest inland waterway and home to over a quarter of the rarest plants and animals in the UK…

# My Norfolk

The Norfolk Broads has many lovely villages along its banks such as Wroxham, Hoveton, Coltishall, Horning and Stalham that are enjoyed all the year round with beautiful scenery and plenty to do. Wroxham, known as the capital of the Norfolk Broads, sits on the bank of the River Bure. Wroxham is the hub for hiring boats for day trips and holidays as well as exploring the Broads National Park. You will also find a narrow-gauge train line running steam and diesel trains to Aylsham as well as a thriving shopping centre. Hoveton is about a mile away from Wroxham and you will find the award winning Bewilderwood, an adventure park with 50 acres of wild, outdoor tree houses and Wroxham Barns with a farm, indoor play area, mini golf, shops and a restaurant close by. A short distance away is the picturesque village of Horning. From here you can also take a trip on the Broads to Ranworth on a double-decked paddle-steamer (see above)…

# My Norfolk

Also on the Norfolk Broads is the historic town of Coltishall which was the centre of the maltings industry for over 200 years and was also home to boat building yards. This is where the famous traditional Norfolk Wherries were made. The town is now the gateway to the Norfolk Broads and is a hive of boating activity in the summer. It also has a renowned tearoom, riverside pubs and a country manor. At the northern end of the Norfolk Broads is Stalham, a small market town by the River Ant which is only four miles from the coast and a fine sandy beach. Stalham has a good range of shops and places to eat, and you can rent boats for breaks on the Norfolk Broads from here. The villages and towns along the Broads National Park offer an ideal base for a holiday any time of the year with stunning scenery and a raft of wildlife. It is ideal for exploring by boat, walking or even on a bike. One of the best sights of the Norfolk Broads is the beautiful swallowtail butterfly (see above) which is the largest butterfly to be found in the UK. When out and about remember to stop off at one of the many fine local pubs along the way for a fine meal and great local beers…

# My Norfolk

## Acle

Acle is a flourishing market town with some very attractive 17th and 18th century buildings and a church which is more than 900 years old. It is situated 10 miles east of Norwich and 8 miles west of Great Yarmouth and has good rail connections to both places. A produce market is held here every Thursday but it is vastly different from the traditional livestock market of years gone by. Acle is considered to be one of the main gateways to the Norfolk Broads and it is the starting point for many of the Broads boating holidays. Two miles from the town is Acle Bridge where there are two boatyards which offer boat hire. The bridge also has an excellent view of the River Bure. Above we see a Norfolk Wherry sailing on the Norfolk Broads near Acle. The annual Acle Sailing Regatta takes place just west of the bridge, in May each year, and attracts sailing boats from all across the Norfolk Broads and beyond…

# My Norfolk

## Attleborough

The history of Attleborough can be traced right back to Saxon times. Sadly in 1559, much of the town was destroyed by fire. The traditional industries of turkey-rearing and brush-making still take place in the town today. The turkey is also shown on the town sign. It is said to depict the days when Attleborough turkeys had their feet dipped in tar to withstand the journey along the roads to the London markets. The town's Carnival week takes place in June, when organisations get together to host an array of activities including an excellent parade of floats. The town has a good selection of shops and there is also a weekly market held on Thursdays. Attleborough is twinned with the French town of Nevil les Aubiers…

# My Norfolk

## Aylsham

Aylsham is a bustling market town that stands next to the River Bure. There are many fine 17th and 18th century buildings and an impressive mid-Victorian watermill whose ancestry can be traced back to the Domesday Book in the town. Aylsham was famed for its linen and canvas industry during the 14th century and then later on it became renowned for its weaving of woollen and worstead cloths. Sadly this industry was killed off by the development of the knitting frame. Today the town's market place has stalls trading on most days. The Aylsham Show is held annually in Blickling Park on August Bank Holiday Monday and is one of the largest one-day shows in the country. Nearby the National Trust's Blickling Hall is a magnificent Jacobean house, with stunning gardens. It is believed that Anne Boleyn's ghost still roams the hall of the house! Aylsham is the northern terminus of the Bure Valley Railway, a narrow-gauge steam railway which takes you through the countryside to Wroxham. The station also marks the start of the Bure Valley Walk, a walking and cycling route that runs alongside the railway line…

# My Norfolk

## Blakeney

Blakeney is in an area of outstanding natural beauty and is an ideal base to exploring the north Norfolk coast. At the heart of the area, is the Blakeney National Nature Reserve that has wide open spaces and uninterrupted views of the coastline. It is ideal for walking and seeing wildlife including seals and migratory birds. The village has pretty flint cottages, once home to local fisherman now more likely they are second homes or rentals for the holiday market. There are several places to eat and stay as well as pubs, gift shops and art galleries. A couple of miles walk away is Cley next the Sea with its great views across the marshes and it was on this marshland that they used to hold horse races on up to the early 19th century. Blakeney sands is also home to grey seals and their pups, born during November to early January, and is the largest seal colony in England with over 2,000 seal pups born there annually. The local seaweed delicacy of samphire can also be found growing here in the wild mudflat's and surrounding seashore's…

# My Norfolk

## Brancaster and Brancaster Staithe

Brancaster Staithe and Brancaster are close to each other and just a four mile walk west takes you to Burnham Overy Staithe. Brancaster is a lively village which hosts a Christmas market and has an Outdoor and Wildlife festival in the summer. Brancaster is known for its mussels and excellent seafood which you can try in the eateries or buy from stalls at the staithe or on the main road. The village is renowned for having one of the lowest amounts of rainfall in the country. You can enjoy lots of outdoors activities nearby such as sailing or kite surfing. Brancaster beach is really stunning with miles of un-spoilt golden sand and is also dog friendly. When the tide is out you can see an old shipwreck. This is the remains of SS Vina which was used by the RAF for target practice before the Normandy landings of World War Two…

# My Norfolk

## Burnham Market and Burnham Overy Staithe

**Burnham Market** is the major of the Burnham's, it is a unique traditional Georgian village. It lies just two mile from Brancaster Beach and six miles from Wells-next-the-Sea, and is close to several renowned nature reserves. Around the village green, you will find a boutique, antique shops, eateries and art galleries interspersed with charming cottages. Like the other Burnham's, Burnham Market retains a unique and special village feel, whilst also being a favourite haunt of celebrities. **Burnham Overy Staithe** is very popular with the sailing set, you will find tidal creeks where the river spreads through the salt marshes and sand dunes at Burnham Harbour all the way out to the sea. You can walk the one mile to the beach through the marshes and dunes where you will be rewarded for your effort with golden secluded sands…

# My Norfolk

## Burnham Thorpe

Burnham Thorpe is close to Burnham Market and is famous for being the birthplace of Vice Admiral Horatio Nelson (born: 1758). He was the victor at the Battle of Trafalgar and is one of England's greatest heroes. Nelson's birthplace, The Parsonage, was knocked down in 1803, but in the old grounds you can see the pond that Nelson dug. It is probable that Horatio first saw the sea and ships at Burnham Overy Staithe, and may even have learned to sail thereabouts. In his youth, he would ride to Wells Next The Sea, then a busy sea port, where he would watch the ships come and go, and listen to the sailors' stories. When raised to the peerage in 1798 he took the title Baron Nelson of the Nile and of Burnham Thorpe. In the village is 'The Lord Nelson' pub which Horatio frequented (it was then known as The Plough Inn). The pub is still there today and is much as it was in Nelson's day…

# My Norfolk

## Cley next the Sea

Cley next the Sea was an important trading port in the middle ages and is now best known for its renowned nature reserve. Between the village and the sea, you will finds Cley Marshes, a nature reserve owned by the Norfolk Wildlife Trust 'in perpetuity as a bird breeding sanctuary'. Cley's lagoons, beach, grazing marsh and reed beds attract wintering and migrating wildfowl and waders, making it a haven for bird watchers. Standing on the edge of the marshes and the village is Cley's other famous landmark, an 18th century windmill. Now a guesthouse, it is open to the public offering fantastic views over marshland which was used for horse races in the early 19th century and was also a haunt for smugglers! The shingle beach can be accessed through the marshes and is a great place for sea fishing. The narrow village streets are lined with unique shops including a smokehouse, bookshop, tea shops and a pub as well as a shop selling hand-thrown stoneware pottery, made on site. Cley next the Sea is a tranquil place with a breath taking landscape and is ideal for those wanting to explore the Norfolk coast and its wildlife…

# My Norfolk

## Cromer

The Norfolk town of Cromer is well known for its pier which has a lifeboat station and the Pavilion Theatre, home to the UK's only remaining traditional end of the pier variety show. The pier is an enduring example of Victorian building, having withstood many storms, tidal surges and even an attempt to blow it up by the Government in World War Two to prevent the pier being used as a landing strip for enemy invaders! The lifeboat house is just up a ramp off the beach and Cromer's lifeboat crew are the most decorated in RNLI history. Lifeboat man Henry Blogg, is the most famous person who served for 53 years on Cromer's lifeboats, who, with his crew, saved over 873 lives from the North Sea. Back in the 19th century, the town was developed into a seaside resort by the Victorians. Today, the streets and alleys are bustling with shops, pubs, cafes and restaurants where you can enjoy the famous Cromer crab! All year round, spending time on the beach at Cromer is a must. Have a go at crabbing, building sand castles on the family friendly sands or try surfing and/or paddle boarding…

# My Norfolk

## Dereham

Dereham town market place and high street are full of Georgian buildings and there is still a sense of days gone by behind the modern facades of the shop windows. Every Friday there is a large market offering a good variety of merchandise; a smaller market is held on Tuesdays and a monthly farmers' market is held at the railway station. Dereham has a wide choice of restaurants, pubs and tea-rooms and a good selection of shops. There are sports facilities in the town for tennis, golf, swimming and bowls. It also has a 19th century windmill…

# My Norfolk

## Diss

Diss is a lovely old market town, which has grown up around its great Mere that comes to the very edge of the main shopping street and covers an area of nearly six acres. It is a very pretty town and a pleasant place to spend some time in just wandering around and/or doing some shopping…

# My Norfolk

## Downham Market

Downham Market is one of Norfolk's oldest market towns and is very close to where we live. Its history can be traced right back to Saxon times. Charles I went for refuge to Downham Market following the Battle of Naseby and the inventor George Manby went to school in the town. The town has a range of individual shops and a bustling market that is held in the market square on Fridays and Saturdays. There are many attractive houses and buildings with an unusual black and white clock near the marketplace (see above). David Bellamy, Britain's favourite botanist, once described the nearby Fens as 'a natural man-scape'. The land was covered by water until the huge task of draining the area was undertaken. It is now some of the most fertile farmland in Europe. Downham Market is an ideal area for a walking or cycling holiday as the landscape is so flat and the nearby peaceful waterways are also excellent for boating and fishing holidays. We live in a small village just up the road from the town of Downham Market and shop there regularly…

# My Norfolk

## Fakenham

In the Norfolk town of Fakenham flint tools and weapons have been discovered suggesting that the area was inhabited during the Neolithic period. There is also evidence of a settlement in Roman times on Beacon Hill. The Doomsday Book in 1086 states that Fakenham at that time had a population of 150, vastly different from today's ever-increasing population. The town's market place, which was granted a charter in 1250, is still very much in use today. Wind power was used in the 18th and 19th Centuries in Fakenham, followed by gas and electricity. The town gas works was built in 1845 and Fakenham's gas museum tells the story of how gas was once responsible for lighting up the whole town. In 1862 Thomas Miller built up a prosperous business in book printing, which went from a local operation to a substantial concern supplying books to a variety of major London publishers. Today Fakenham still has its Thursday market and has a small selection of shops like the traditional butchers, bakers and greengrocers that can be found on its streets. Susie and I have happy memories of the town as we were married in Fakenham many years ago!...

# My Norfolk

## Great Yarmouth

Great Yarmouth is the most famous seaside holiday town in Norfolk but for centuries it was also an important fishing port. The town was renowned for the large catches of herrings which were landed at the towns port and cleaned by the Scottish herring fleet girls before being smoked locally. Today visitors can visit one of the old smoke houses for themselves and experience the sights, smells and sounds of this bygone industry for themselves at the Time and Tide museum. Great Yarmouth was founded by the Angles. By the time of the Domesday Book, in 1086, it had grown into a little town with a population of a few hundred. The prosperity of Great Yarmouth was based on herring fishing and by the 12th century a herring fair was held at Yarmouth. The fairs were like markets but they were held only once a year. Merchants came from all over Europe to buy herrings at the Great Yarmouth fair. Apart from fishing there was also a large shipbuilding industry to be found in Great Yarmouth. Today holidaymakers and day trippers can still take a traditional donkey ride or make sand castles on the towns long golden soft sands!…

# My Norfolk

## Great Yarmouth

Great Yarmouth was also an important port for trade with Europe due to its position close to the coast of Holland. The herring fishing industry reached a peak at the start of the 20th century. However it then went into a relentless decline. Meanwhile, from the end of the 18th century Great Yarmouth developed as a seaside holiday resort. In those days people believed that bathing in the sea was good for your health. Spending time at the seaside became fashionable with the well off. Great Yarmouth developed still more when the railway reached the town in 1844. Today Great Yarmouth continues to be an important and flourishing resort. In 2010 a new deep water harbour was opened. The population today of Great Yarmouth is in the region of 47,000. Today the town has a golden mile long promenade, kiss me quick hats, a large fun fare, a horse racing course as well as a dog racing track and much, much more…

# My Norfolk

# Happisburgh

Happisburgh is home to the oldest working lighthouse in the county and the only independently operated lighthouse in the UK. The famous red and white striped lighthouse was built in 1790 and offers wonderful views of the coast and countryside. In the summer, it is open to visitors on occasional Sundays. In the area coastal erosion is constantly changing the landscape of the shoreline at Happisburgh. This has revealed evidence of humans being present in Great Britain 200,000 years earlier than had previously been known. Flint axes and early fossilized human footprints found here date back over 800,000 years and are the oldest evidence of man that has been found outside of the Great Rift Valley in Africa! These finds, as well as the mammoth skeleton uncovered by cliff erosion in West Runton near Cromer, have earned this coastline the name, the Deep History Coast. The secluded, sandy beach at Happisburgh is dog friendly and great for family days out. We often take our dogs there and from the beach, you can walk as far as Sea Palling taking in the wonderful sea views along the way. Happisburgh is a pretty village and an ideal base for a north Norfolk holiday to remember…

# My Norfolk

## Holkham

Holkham is home to a 25,000 acre estate on the north Norfolk coast, in which stands Holkham Hall, an 18th century Palladian house, home to the Earl of Leicester. Surrounding the house is rolling parkland that has fallow deer and red deer roaming free. The un-spoilt picturesque beach at Holkham nearby, has expansive white sand backed by sand dunes and pine woods. The setting is popular with walkers and bathers alike, it can feel almost empty even in the height of summer. Behind the shoreline lies a basin, which, at high tides, fills to form a spectacular shallow lagoon. Holkham beach is also part of one of the largest National Nature Reserves in the country and is home to many rare and endangered species of flora and fauna…

# My Norfolk

## Holt

Holt is a beautiful Georgian country town set in the North Norfolk countryside. It is a few miles from the coast and is connected to the coastal town of Sheringham by the North Norfolk Railway. In the town there are quaint streets and courtyards that house bookshops, antique, bric-a-brac shops, art galleries and many other shops that sell unusual and interesting goods. Many of the shops are family run businesses, which offer that special personal service sadly missing in the majority of shops today. Holt in the summer has an almost continental atmosphere, with many of its pubs and restaurants providing outside seating. The town in the winter is reminiscent of a traditional Christmas card scene with twinkling white lights fitted to every building in sight. Just outside the centre of Holt is the North Norfolk Railway station where you can catch the Poppy Line steam and/or diesel train services to Weybourne and Sheringham. A regular bus service runs between the train station and Holt's market place. Holt's rural coastal location, with its unique town centre, makes it the ideal place to visit or stay in at any time of the year…

# My Norfolk

Susie on the beach at Hunstanton…

## Hunstanton

The Norfolk town of Hunstanton was purpose-built by local landowner Henry Styleman le Strange in 1846. It is affectionately known locally today as "Sunny Hunny" as it has some of the driest sunniest weather in the UK. The town is built mainly in Norfolk carrstone and has many attractive buildings. The resort features a fabulous sandy beach and the famous striped cliffs of Hunstanton. In the resort there is a sea life centre, fun fair, amusement arcades, bowls, crazy golf, pitch & putt and even pony rides on the beach in the summer with of course buckets, spades and candy floss for the little ones. The town has excellent wind conditions for sailing, windsurfing and kite surfing for those who enjoy more exhilarating outdoor pursuits. The town also boasts an excellent leisure centre offering a well-equipped fitness suite, a tropical pool with slide and giant inflatables, squash, bowls and a soft play area for toddlers. Boat trips in the summer takes visitors out to sea for a closer look at the local seals and birds in their natural habitat. Susie, our dogs Poppy and Charlie and I often go to Hunstanton beach for a long walk mainly in the winter months to avoid the crowds!…

# My Norfolk

## Kings Lynn

Kings Lynn was once called Bishops Lynn because it belonged to a Bishop (Bishops Lynn became Kings Lynn in the 16th century). The word Lynn means pool and probably refers to a tidal pool on the river Ouse. By the end of the 11th century a little trading settlement grew up there. King's Lynn, in West Norfolk, is a medieval port steeped in maritime history, which stands on the River Ouse. In medieval times it was considered a very important port and was only exceeded by the ports of London and Southampton. Its trade brought great wealth to the area and many fine buildings were built in the town. The town was protected by walls and gatehouses and the South Gatehouse is still standing today. Susie and I live just six miles outside Kings Lynn in the small West Norfolk village of Shouldham…

# My Norfolk

# Kings Lynn

Kings Lynn town centre has a Saturday and a Tuesday market place and they have been in use for more than 900 years. In 1349 the Black Death struck the town and nearly half of the town's population perished. The town also suffered great loss of life when floods and gales caused shipping disasters. The town's Trinity Guildhall is the home of 'Tales of the Old Gaol House'. Visitors can see the original cells of the town's jail and listen to the corresponding information by personal stereo. In 1683 the magnificent Custom House was built, which is now home to the town's Tourist Information Centre. It also houses a special display of the town's maritime history. Kings Lynn is also a thriving shopping town with three weekly markets. Like all Tudor and Stuart towns Kings Lynn suffered from outbreaks of plague. There were severe outbreaks in 1516, 1587, 1597, 1636 and 1665. But thankfully the 1665 outbreak proved to be the last. Fire was another major hazard so in 1572 thatched roofs were banned in the town to reduce the risk of fire in the houses in Kings Lynn…

# My Norfolk

## Kings Lynn

In Kings Lynn in 1642 the English civil war between the King and parliament came to the town. At first Kings Lynn supported parliament but in August 1643 after a change in government the town changed sides. Parliament lost no time in sending an army to capture the town. Kings Lynn was besieged for 3 weeks before it surrendered. By the early 17th century Kings Lynn had ceased to be a major international port although some iron, timber and pitch were still imported through the port. Like other ports on the East Coast Kings Lynn suffered from the discovery of the Americas, which obviously benefited ports on the west coast of the UK. It was also affected by the growth of the ports in London which tended to 'suck in' trade. However in the late 17th century imports of wine from Spain, Portugal and France into Kings Lynn boomed…

# My Norfolk

## Kings Lynn

In the middle of the 17th century the nearby fens were drained and turned into farmland. As a result vast amounts of farm produce were exported from Kings Lynn to the growing market in London. Furthermore Kings Lynn was still an important fishing port. By the late 17th century shipbuilding had become an important industry in Kings Lynn. A glass making industry also began in the late 17th century. In 1683 an architect named Henry Bell, who was once lord mayor of Kings Lynn, built the Custom House. In the 18th century shipbuilding continued to thrive in Kings Lynn. So did associated industries such as sail and rope making and glass making continued to prosper. Brewing was another important industry in Kings Lynn. The first bank in Kings Lynn opened in 1784. In 1801 the population of Kings Lynn was 10,096. It grew rapidly to about 20,000 in 1851. Then the population actually fell to around 17,000 in 1871. Thereafter the population of Kings Lynn grew again but this time very slowly…

# My Norfolk

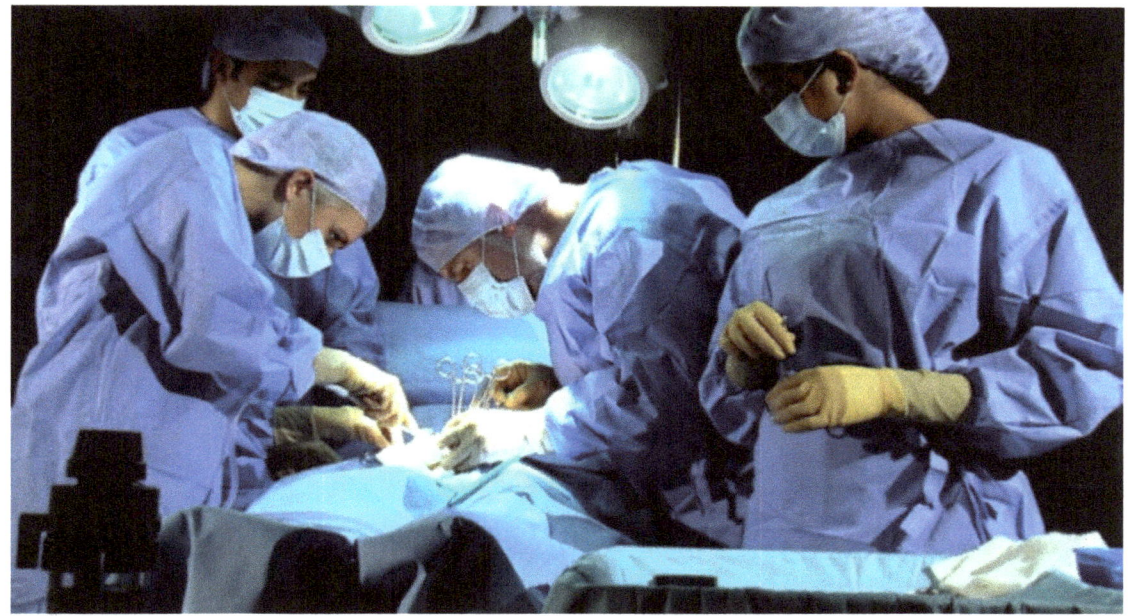

## Kings Lynn

There were a number of improvements to Kings Lynn in the 19th century. In 1803 and 1806 acts of parliament formed a body of men with powers to pave, clean and light the streets. In 1813 a dispensary was founded where the poor could obtain free medicines. The Lynn and West Norfolk hospital was opened in 1835. Today the Queen Elizabeth II hospital now serves the people of the town and it's surrounding area. I had both of my knee replacement operations performed here by Mr. James Jeffery recently and Susie has also safely undergone two major surgery procedures here in the last few years. We are both very grateful to all of the hospital staff for taking such good care of us both. Meanwhile, back to the past and a Corn Exchange (where grain could be bought and sold) was built in 1854. Public Baths were built in 1856. The County Court was built in 1861 and a Technical school opened in Kings Lynn in 1893. Meanwhile the railway reached Kings Lynn in 1847. Then in the late 19th century a network of sewers and a proper public water supply was created. The port of Kings Lynn continued to thrive in the 19th century. Amenities in Kings Lynn continued to improve in the 20th century. A museum opened in Kings Lynn in 1904. A public library opened in 1905. The first moving pictures were shown in Kings Lynn in 1910. The Majestic Cinema opened in 1928. Then in the 1930's the town council began a programme of slum clearance…

# My Norfolk

## Kings Lynn

When World War II began it was assumed that Kings Lynn would be safe from bombing and many evacuees were sent there from London. However Kings Lynn was not completely safe and suffered several air raids. Most of the evacuees soon returned home. In 1962 it was agreed that Kings Lynn should become an overflow town for London. The old industry of brewing died out by the 1950's but new industries came to Kings Lynn. From the 1930's there was a food canning industry in the town and from the 1950's soup making. In the 1960's the council tried to attract new industries by building a new industrial estate at Hardwick. The new industries included light engineering, clothes and chemicals. Fishing remained an important industry. Today tourism is also important to the town. True's Yard Fishing Museum opened in 1991 and the Town House Museum opened in 1992. In 2003 a new skate and bike park opened. Today the population of Kings Lynn is 42,000. Susie and I go into Kings Lynn every week to do our weekly food shopping…

# My Norfolk

Alan in the Norfolk sunshine…

## Mundesley

The Norfolk coastal village of Mundesley became popular with the Victorians, when visitors were brought to the area with the opening of a railway line to the resort in 1889. Today the railway has long gone, but the sandy beach and fresh sea breezes off the North Sea still attract many visitors to the resort. Mundesley has a wide sandy beach, with colourful beach huts and shallow rock pools that are an ideal playground for children of all ages. The charming village has pretty cottages, shops, pubs, places to eat with pretty thatched buildings and flint stone walls. Mundesley is also home to a Maritime Museum, believed to be one of the smallest museums in England! Opposite the museum is a World War II memorial to the men who were killed while clearing landmine's from the cliffs and beaches after the war. Mundesley is perfect for those seeking a traditional seaside holiday, scenic walks and family friendly activities…

# My Norfolk

Poppy in the long grass...

## North Walsham

The Norfolk market town of North Walsham, became a centre for weaving in the Anglo-Saxon era, along with the nearby village of Worstead (from where the cloth gets its name). North Walsham is situated six miles from the coast and nine miles from the Norfolk Broads. North Walsham is an ancient town that had a settlement in Saxon time. The charter of King Edward also indicates that a church was there before the Norman Conquest of 1066. Market day is on Thursday, which was originally granted by Henry III. During June a Medieval Fair takes place, which is a fun-packed day out for all the family. North Walsham is situated on the Bittern Line railway, providing easy access to the nearby north Norfolk coast. The Weaver's Way footpath also runs through the town for those who want to explore the surrounding area on cycle or on foot…

# My Norfolk

## Reepham

The Norfolk town of Reepham that dates back to just after the Norman Conquest, has beautiful 18th century buildings lining pretty streets and alleys. The town is home to some shops, a 16th century pub as well as plenty of other places to eat. Reepham market was founded in 1277 when Sir John de Vaux obtained a charter from King Edward I. Today, the market place, a conservation area, holds a country market on Wednesday mornings, as well as frequent antiques fairs. Reepham Station is the start of the Marriott's Way trail. It is perfect for cycling, walking and horse riding, the 21 miles of former railway track-bed, takes you to Whitwell Station on the outskirts of Reepham. There you will find a museum, old station buildings, rolling stock and frequent steam train events. Just 12 miles from Norwich and 16 miles from Mundesley beach, Reepham is surrounded by countryside and is ideal for a walking holiday and for those who want to just wander around an old traditional Norfolk market town…

# My Norfolk

## Sea Palling

Sea Palling is a quiet village on the north Norfolk coast with an award winning beach and unique areas of un-spoilt natural beauty. The beach is ideal for children with safe seawater calmed by man-made coastal defence reefs. Sea Palling has a rich history dominated by sea flooding, ship wrecks and heroism on the waves. Along the coastline, you will find sand dunes separating the low lying land from the sea. The dunes offer amazing views of the surrounding Norfolk coast and countryside. Nearby Waxham has a sandy beach, and is a wonderful location to spot seals close in-shore, and in the winter, the seals can be seen on the beach with their pups. The village is also home to one of the largest and most famous 16th century tithe barns in the country, with a small exhibition of Elizabethan agriculture and a cafe. For a quiet traditional holiday with a traditional Norfolk village feel, Sea Palling is a good choice and offers great access to the coast and the Norfolk countryside…

# My Norfolk

## Sheringham

The coastal town of Sheringham is on the North Norfolk coast and, up until the late 19th Century, it was just a small fishing village boasting nearly 150 boats. The fishermen brought ashore catches such as cod, whiting and skate, as well as crabs and lobsters, which the town is renowned for today. In 1887 the rail link arrived which meant that the number of holiday visitors to the town greatly increased. Sheringham is a busy town with a good variety of family run shops and a very popular market. The beach is mostly shingle and is a great spot for bathing. Sheringham also has the North Norfolk Railway that runs from the old Sheringham train station, through Weybourne and on to the town of Holt. A must do for train/steam enthusiasts. It is an ideal way of seeing the beautiful Norfolk coastline and surrounding countryside. The town of Sheringham is an ideal base for a traditional seaside family holiday or for a long weekend break to enjoy the north Norfolk coast and the surrounding countryside…

# My Norfolk

## Swaffham

Swaffham is a very pretty Norfolk market town with many fine Georgian buildings scattered around the central town market place. Susie and I live just a few miles away in a small village called Shouldham. The Butter Cross is an interesting feature and is situated in the market place itself. It was erected in 1783 and comprises of eight stone columns and a dome featuring a figure of the Goddess Ceres. On the town sign the legendary "Pedlar of Swaffham", John Chapman, is depicted. Figures of John and his wife are also carved on a bench end that is within the spectacular town parish church. The local history museum has exhibits dating back to the Stone Age as well as a Howard Carter King Tutankhamun display and is well worth a visit. Howard Carter who discovered the tomb and the fabulous treasure of the ancient Egyptian boy King Tutankhamun parents Samuel and Martha were both Swaffham people. They had eleven children of whom Howard was the youngest. Howard Carter spent much of his childhood and teenage years in and around the town of Swaffham. The towns large and vibrant market is held in the market place every Saturday throughout the year…

# My Norfolk

## Thetford

Thetford and it's surrounding area is the earliest settlement in Norfolk. The famous Stone Age flint mines at Grimes Graves is just north of the town and there is evidence that there was much activity in the area during the Neolithic period. Gallows Hill is where a huge find of gold and silver was uncovered, as well as the remains of a temple. Thetford was a main stopping point on the coaching road from London. Many of the coaching hotels in the town can still be seen today with their wide archway doorways enabling the horse drawn coaches to make their entrance. After the Second World War the main London road stopped running through the town centre, when a by-pass was created. Thetford Castle Hill is England's tallest medieval earthwork. In the town the ruins of a Cluniac priory and Benedictine nunnery can be seen, as well as a timber framed building that houses the local history museum (see above). The Market Place may appear familiar to 'Dad's Army' enthusiasts as the Guildhall was used as the set for the famous Walmington on Sea's town hall in the popular television series…

# My Norfolk

## (Little) Walsingham

Just four miles inland from Wells-next-the-Sea, on the banks of the River Stiffkey, is the village of Little Walsingham. It has a long history of religious pilgrimage and has a wealth of historic buildings. The history of Walsingham and its pilgrimages began in the 11th century with the visions of the Virgin Mary by the lady Walsingham, Richeldis de Faverches. She requested that a replica of the Holy House at Nazareth be built at Little Walsingham. This became 'England's Nazareth', a place of prayer and reconciliation and one of Europe's four great pilgrim sites in the Middle Ages. The pilgrimage season at Walsingham runs from Easter to the end of October. In the village, you can see many 14th and 15th century buildings. You will also find plenty of shops in the pretty little village including tea rooms and cafes. Little Walsingham is also home to the Wells and Walsingham Light Railway, said to be the longest 10-and-a-quarter inch narrow-gauge steam railway in the world…

# My Norfolk

## Watton

The Norfolk town of Watton is 21 miles west of the City of Norwich, with the Norfolk Broads and the east coast not far beyond. In Watton High Street there is an unusual clock tower, which dates from 1679. This was erected after a fire destroyed much of the town in 1674, the clock was installed reputedly so that its bells could warn townsfolk should such a disaster strike again. On the Watton town sign there are the two 'babes' from the popular fairytale "Babes in the Woods". It is said that the nearby Wayland Wood is where the two 'babes in the wood' unfortunately met their fate. The hare (wat) and barrel (tun) also feature on the town sign showing the derivation of the town's name. Today the town of Watton has a thriving community with a bustling high street where you can purchase the locally made 'Wayland Sausage' and 'Wayland Bap'. Wednesday is market day with an additional farmers' market also held in the town on the first Saturday of every month…

# My Norfolk

## Wells Next the Sea

Located between the world-renowned Holkham beach and the unique bird sanctuary of Blakeney Point, lies the pretty harbour town of Wells Next the Sea. It is Susie and my favourite Norfolk seaside resort. Its harbour is sheltered by salt marshes from the open sea and was once one of the great ports of eastern England in Tudor times. Today the harbour is still used by sailing and crabbing boats and is overlooked by an imposing granary building dating from 1904. The town of Wells Next the Sea has a leafy Georgian Square and on Staithe Street you will find a mix of traditional and contemporary shops. On the outskirts of town, is a light railway which takes you on a four mile train ride to Little Walsingham. You can walk from the town to the sandy beach, or take the seasonal narrow-gauge railway. There you can take a walk through shady pinewoods to the sandy beach, and you'll be greeted with a row of colourful beach huts and may also get to see seals basking on the sand banks out to sea. Wells Next the Sea and nearby Holkham offer the perfect setting for a north Norfolk holiday to remember…

# My Norfolk

## Wymondham

The town of Wymondham is a delightful Norfolk market town with a market cross that was re-built after suffering fire damage in 1615. There are many fine 17th and 18th century houses scattered along the winding streets and an imposing abbey with two towers, one at each end, which look somewhat unfinished with their plain tops. This is a great place to wander around and visit the many shops and historic buildings to be found on the main town shopping street that leads up to the historic market cross…

# My Norfolk

## The City of Norwich

I was born in the City of Norwich in 1949 some seventy one years ago! Norwich is a beautiful city, steeped in history, dating back over 2,000 years. The central streets still follow their medieval course outlined by what remains of the ancient city walls. Norwich is dominated by its magnificent Cathedral and medieval Castle. The city's newest public building, The Forum, is also an impressive landmark, situated in the heart of the city centre, offering information and entertainment. From its historic buildings and beautiful courtyards, to outstanding modern architecture and stunning parks, there is something here for the whole family. Norwich is rated in the top ten of UK shopping destinations. Norwich is also a great place for a night out, with a mix of trendy pubs, clubs, cinemas and restaurants, and stylish café bars. Art lovers, film buffs and theatre-goers will not be disappointed by the excellent choices on offer in this vibrant city. Norwich is overflowing with a diversity of entertainment that will suit every conceivable taste and budget. It is also home to my football team Norwich City Football Club. Norwich is an ancient city that lies at the heart of rural East Anglia. It was the Anglo Saxons who first made their homes beside the river Wensum, and it was from one of these settlements, which bore the name Northwic, that the city got its name. In time it grew into a town, perhaps because of its situation on a river. (In those days it was much cheaper and easier to transport goods for sale by water than by land). It became known as North Wic (wic is an Old Saxon word for port and Norwich was after all an inland port)…

# My Norfolk

## The City of Norwich

The name Norwich first appears on a coin minted in the early 10th century. By then Norwich was a large and important town. It had a mint and would have had a weekly market. Norwich was probably also a burgh or fortified settlement. The town would have been surrounded by a ditch and earth embankment with a wooden palisade on top. In the 10th century The City of Norwich grew rapidly. Featured above is the oldest pub in Norwich called the Adam and Eve. This pub is special to me as this is where I first went with my now wife Susie for a lunchtime meal. We had first met when we were serving as jurors on Jury service in February 1993 at the Norwich Crown Court. I was living, on my own, at the time, in a small terrace house on Vincent Road at the top of Ketts Hill which is not to far away from the centre of Norwich. We later moved to a small Norfolk village called East Lexham were we got married in Fakenham and later moved to were we live now in the west Norfolk village of Shouldham. Meanwhile as the town of Norwich grew the settlement spread to the south bank of the river. Gradually the settlement at Norwich shifted from north to south of the river Wensum. Then in 1004 the Danes sacked and burned Norwich. That was easy since the buildings were of wood with thatched roofs at that time. However, the town of Norwich was soon rebuilt and flourished once again. The Danes left many place names in this part of England. The street name 'gate', as in Pottergate, is derived from the Danish word gata meaning street. Potter gata was the street where potters lived and worked. The meaning of Fishergate is obvious. The street name of Tombland is derived from a Danish word meaning empty space. The street name of Fingelgate comes from a Danish word meaning bend or elbow…

# My Norfolk

## The City of Norwich

The settlement of Norwich grew and grew and merged with other small villages to become the largest walled town in medieval England. In 1066, at the time of the Norman Conquest, Norwich was one of the most important boroughs in the Kingdom. Trade by river and sea was increasing and light industry had begun to develop. The market on Tombland was thriving with local produce, pottery, ironwork, wooden and leather goods, as well as furs from Scandinavia and Russia, woollen cloth from Flanders and herring from the North Sea. Norwich Castle was built by the Norman Conquerors as a show of strength. A steep-sided artificial hill was constructed in 1067 which was 40 feet (13 metres) above ground level. Originally the castle was made of wood and was replaced 60 years later by a stone keep, which can still be seen today. The keep was roughly 70 feet (20 metres) high, with walls about 100 feet (30 metres) long, and was virtually square in shape. It was built of local flint and mortar, and faced with stone. Built by the Normans in the 12th century. Norwich Castle is one of the finest Norman secular buildings to be found in Europe. Originally built as a royal palace, the castle is now a museum and art gallery, packed with treasures and collections of national importance. The archaeology gallery has displays about Queen Boudica, with a ride-on re-creation of an Iceni warrior's chariot. There is an Egyptian collection which is displayed in a replica Egyptian tomb with ancient mummies. For spectacular views over Norwich, you can climb up to the battlements, and also take a tour of the dungeons. In the cells you get a real feel for what life was really like for prisoners who were incarcerated here in years gone by …

# My Norfolk

## The City of Norwich

In 1096 building work started on the Norwich Cathedral and many Saxon houses were cleared so that a canal could be dug from the River Wensum to the site of the Cathedral. This meant that stone from Caen in Normandy could be brought directly to the building site by water, thus making lighter work. By 1119 the transepts, presbytery and four bays of the nave had been built, but the Cathedral was not finally consecrated until 1278. The magnificent Cathedral dominates the city skyline. Situated in the heart of the city, Norwich Cathedral has attracted many pilgrims and visitors for over 900 years. Separated from the busy streets by flint walls and entrance gates, it is a place of great splendour and tranquillity and has at least three services daily. In the Medieval times the city of Norwich had within its walls 56 churches. Many of these were built as a reflection of wealth of local landowners. In 1194 Norwich became a city when Richard I granted a charter giving rights of self-government. 1349 was when The Black Death hit Norwich and it is thought that as many as two-fifths of the population of roughly 6,000 people may have died. With a high proportion of clergy dying, four parish churches fell into disuse because of the lack of priests and parishioners. However, by 1377, Norwich's, population had risen back to 6,000. Many of the new residents were peasants who had left their unproductive land to seek work in the city's growing textile trade. At the beginning of the 14th century, weaving was the most important trade in the city and, within a hundred years, Norwich was considered the main centre of worsted manufacture in the country. This industry continued for the next five hundred years until machinery was introduced during the Industrial Revolution thus making skilled craftsmen redundant. The Peasants' Revolt of 1381 meant life at the end of the 14th century was far from peaceful. Armies of rebels set fire to the houses of lawyers and other wealthy people and it was the bishop, who, with his own army, eventually managed to restore order in the city…

# My Norfolk

## The City of Norwich

During the early 16th century there were several fires which swept through Norwich, destroying whole streets of thatched and Tudor timbered houses. It is thought that 718 houses were burnt to the ground over a four day period in March 1507, and in June of the same year an additional 360 homes were lost to fire. This was almost half of the city's housing stock, which led to a decision that all new buildings in Norwich should have tiled roofs. In 1549 an army of 20,000 rebels, led by Wymondham farmer Robert Kett, took over control of the city; causing a lot of destruction, they were protesting about an increase in rent and the enclosure of local common land for grazing by rich sheep farmers. They made their camp on Mousehold Heath and it took two royal armies six weeks to defeat them. Kett and forty eight other rebels were hanged at Norwich Castle. In 1565 there was great concern about the decline in the worsted industry. The city authorities arranged for thirty households of religious refugees to come over from the Netherlands to teach the local craftsmen how to produce different types of cloth. Not only did the 'Strangers' (as they were known) bring over their knowledge of weaving, they also brought with them a love of gardening and canary breeding. The name the canaries was later to become the nickname of the local Norwich City football team. In Norwich by the end of the 16th century the weaving trade was busy and cloth merchants and grocers were making their fortunes. The local gentry could now buy medicines, imported food and fine clothes without travelling to London. Norwich seemed to be prospering again; however, according to the mayor, in 1570 about a fifth of the population were living on charity and the city was rife with tramps. Norwich experienced its last epidemic of Bubonic Plague during 1665-6; this resulted in most of the wealthy citizens leaving Norwich. Unemployment became a serious problem, followed by a severe food shortage in 1666, which was only averted by huge catches of herring which were brought ashore at Great Yarmouth on the Norfolk coast. Agricultural wages in East Anglia were poor and life became increasingly difficult and prompted people to move once more from the country into the city in search of work…

# My Norfolk

## The City of Norwich

In Norwich the textile industry was recovering from a slump as new interest in fashion meant there were employment opportunities for many. Norwich was now exporting its cloth to Europe, North America, India and China. By the early 1670's Norwich had a population of around 21,000 and was probably the largest provincial town in England. Improvements to the main roads and the development of horse-drawn coaches meant that travelling between towns became easier in the 17th and 18th centuries. The gentry of Norfolk and Suffolk would come into Norwich to make purchases and to take part in social events such as card playing and dancing. During the 18th century Norwich's leather industry steadily grew, making such items as buckets, harnesses, hosepipe's, boots and shoes. Brewing also became increasingly important and Norfolk malting barley was considered the best in the country. By 1801 the city had six large breweries, supplying local needs, as well as sending beer to London for sale. Improvements in local agriculture meant an increased production and a new cattle market grew up around the Castle. Norwich's first bank was opened in 1756 and it was in 1775 that a local family, John and Henry Gurney, started a bank which still survives today as part of Barclays Bank. It was in 1792 that Thomas Bignold, a wine merchant and banker, started the insurance business which was to become Norwich Union. The prosperity meant there was money to invest in building work and the Assembly House was built in 1754. The original Norfolk and Norwich hospital was constructed in 1771-2. During the 19th century the population of Norwich increased from 37,256 in 1811 to 80,368 in 1871. The city began to expand beyond its walls and the living conditions were somewhat unhealthy; with no supply of clean water there were epidemics of cholera and various other deadly diseases. This improved when a new waterworks was built which provided filtered water, and generally people's awareness of public health increased…

# My Norfolk

## The City of Norwich

Norwich originally had three railway stations, but only Thorpe Station, which was opened in 1844, remains today. The meadow land around Thorpe Station soon became crowded with houses and hotels for the railway workers, and factories were built beside the river to take advantage of water and rail transportation. Professional people began building their homes outside the city walls, as the city centre was becoming overcrowded. The area between Ber Street and King Street was particularly over-populated with slum housing. In 1892 work began on the church of St John the Baptist, which was later to become the Roman Catholic Cathedral. It was in the 19th century that Jeremiah Colman built a new mustard mill at Carrow, A.J. Caley began making chocolates at Chapelfield and John Jarrold opened his printing works at Whitefriars. During the 20th century the city's population increased from 121,490 in 1911 to an estimated 180,000 in 1980. Re-housing schemes and slum clearance began in the late 19th century and continued for many years, with council houses providing improved living conditions for thousands of the people of Norwich. From 1900 to 1935 electric trams ran in Norwich but they were later replaced by buses. The first cinema in Norwich opened in 1912. James Stuart Garden opened in 1922. Bridewell Museum opened in 1925. A war memorial was erected in 1927. Woodrow Piling Park opened in 1929. Waterloo Park opened in 1933. The City Hall was built in 1938. The council built houses on the outskirts of Norwich in the 1920's and 1930's. Many more were built after 1945. They were needed partly because 3,000 houses had been damaged or destroyed by German bombing. A new central library was built in 1962 but it burned down in 1994 but it was re-built again in 2002. Norwich University was founded in 1963. The Arts Centre opened in 1977. Anglia Square shopping centre opened in 1980. The Castle Mall shopping centre opened in 1993. The Riverside Leisure Complex opened in 1999. In the late 20th century the main industries in Norwich were printing, electronics, engineering and finance…

# My Norfolk

## The City of Norwich

In the 21st century Norwich is a thriving city. Norwich International Airport is just over 3 miles north of the city centre of Norwich in Norfolk. For many years Norwich International Airport has had flights into the very busy Dutch Airport of Schiphol, and it is increasing its choice of destinations within the UK and Europe. As well as commercial flights, charter helicopters also operate out of Norwich International Airport, flying to North Sea gas rigs. Flying tuition is also permitted at Norwich International Airport and I have personally had a flying lesson at the Norwich International airfield . In the city itself in 2002 a building called The Forum was opened right in the centre of the city and houses the local TV station and it also includes the Millennium Library. Then in 2005 The Chapelfield Shopping Centre was opened. Today the population of the Fine City of Norwich is 132,000. I am very proud to be a Norwich Boy and my team Norwich City Football Club were promoted in 2015 and again in the year (2019) back to the Premier League and now in 2020, just like Norfolk, they are back, I believe, where they belong once more as probably the best team in the best county in the UK. As we leave My Norfolk and move onto the next chapter in which I will share with you my memories of living in the beautiful County of Norfolk…

# My Memories of Norfolk

What follows in this chapter are my personal memories of my early years, my school years, my teenage years, my working/family years and my reflections on my retirement years in the wonderful county of Norfolk.

Alan...

The best thing about being born, raised and living my whole life in Norfolk has been the genuine kindness and generosity of the Norfolk people that I have encountered throughout my long and happy life. I have enjoyed all of the varied vistas of natural beauty, the counties magnificent flora and fauna all framed within the wide open landscape and coastline seascapes which have

# My Memories of Norfolk

## The Early Years (Aged 1 day - 5 years)

I was born in the City of Norwich in Norfolk and like most people I have very little memory of my early years other than brief glimpses and memories of a very happy childhood. What I do remember is being taken to the local parks to toddle in and the local river to paddle in and I also have vague memories of travelling on steam trains. The pictured below is of Wells Next the Sea station and a pre-fabricated bungalow in the early 60's. I remember that we went as a family to the seaside often. I can still remember carrying my bucket and spade onto the beach to make sand castles in the soft golden sand at Great Yarmouth.

Alan and my sister Doreen

I also remember people living in pre-fabricated bungalows (see above) that were built as temporary housing immediately after the second world war (so my mum said) many of which are still being lived in today! Apparently we lived in one for a short period before moving into a brand new council house in West Earlham which is just on the outskirts of the city…

# My Memories of Norfolk

# The School Years (Aged 6 years - 16 years)

The famous black Norfolk turkey's…

Alan aged 9…

During my school years what I remember most of all about those distant years, is that children were allowed to enjoy their childhood and not grow up too quickly. When I think of my younger days, I remembered school for all the opportunities I had to play sport, make things in woodwork and for my first painting experiences in art lessons. I also still have fond memories of playing football at the local park with my friends Phillip. Brian, Gerald, Bernie, Colin, Pip and Peanut to name but a few. These were very happy memories and I spent many a happy school holidays with my uncle Frank, Aunty Joyce and Cousin Beryl at North Creake and being taken by my parents to such places as Lowestoft, Great Yarmouth, Cromer, Sheringham and Wells Next the Sea by steam train from the Norwich train station…

# My Memories of Norfolk

## The Teenage Years (Aged 13 years - 19 years)

When I was a teenager, I was the proud owner of a Vespa scooter that was my pride and joy. I would spend hours cleaning the front and rear chrome carriers and side panels until they sparkled. My friend Bernie also had a scooter, and we spent a lot of time riding around the city of Norwich, going out into the country and parading along Great Yarmouth's Golden Mile on our scooters. We often went down to Hemsby on our scooters for barbecues on the beach and all night parties. The great thing about these machines is that you were never short of having a pretty young thing riding behind you as you toured around. I also have found memories of playing football for North Creake and scoring some great goals (or so I say). Other fond memories are of spending time with my sister Phyllis and her husband Dennis and going to Norwich City football matches and dances with my friends to see the top bands of my day like The Kinks, The Beatles, The Who and many, many more top groups. I count myself as being so very lucky to have been a teenager in the 1960's. Yes - unlike so many who would have loved to have been there I really WAS there!…

# My Memories of Norfolk

# The Family Years (Aged 20 years - 53 years)

It is amazing how quickly your priorities change when you become a husband and a father of your own children. A very sad farewell had to go to my Vespa and the order of the day was for a family car so we could take our children out to the coast, other attractions and places around Norfolk. Like so many of our time we holidayed in caravans and cabins in many of the coastal resorts covered in this book and enjoyed many a sunny Norfolk day making sand castles in the golden sand on the beaches of Norfolk.

My children Mandy and Paul…

The making of sand castles out of the golden sands of Great Yarmouth, Cromer, Wells Next The Sea or any of the many other fine golden sandy beaches around Norfolk with my children Mandy and Paul is still one of my fondest memories from my family years. As a family we did ventured abroad as the children got older but still went on family day trips all around the Norfolk coast regularly…

# My Memories of Norfolk

## My Retirement Years (Aged 54 years - 70 years and counting)

Alan and two of my watercolour paintings...

In 1993 my wife Susie and I moved out of the city of Norwich to a little West Norfolk village called East Lexham in the very heart of Norfolk. The village was so very peaceful and pretty. This helped inspire me to take up watercolour painting. In 2004 we moved to another small West Norfolk village called Shouldham near Downham Market where we still live today. In 2008 I had to take early retirement due to ill health (bad knees). While waiting, undergoing and recovering from having both my knees replaced I continued to garden, paint in watercolours regularly and also started writing. To-date I have been lucky enough to have had paperback and hardback books published on such topics as Gardening, Art, History and Travel. Getting to the age of retirement has meant that I spend most of my time these days enjoying the sunshine and flowers in my Norfolk garden but I still enjoy, from time to time, visiting such places as Wells Next the Sea, Blakeney, Hunstanton and the inland towns of Dereham, Swaffham, Downham Market and Kings Lynn. Up until fairly recently we have also enjoyed having summer fortnight holidays to the Greek paradise island of Skiathos. However, there is still nothing I like more than to be sitting with my paint brushes, watercolour paints and paper by the North Norfolk coast painting while watching the birds in the sky and the sea breaking on the shoreline. Retirement for me has been a great joy and being able to share this special time in my life with Susie makes every day special for me!...

## My Memories of Norfolk

## Some of the my favourite images of Norfolk

Harvest time, Norwich marketplace, beach huts at Wells, a field of poppies and a field of mustard seed flowers

Having shared some of my personal memories of growing up in Norfolk with you it is now time for us, in the next chapter, to have a wander around **My Village**…

# My Village

Hello my name is Alan and I am married to Susie, we live in the beautiful Norfolk village of Shouldham in England in the UK. We have lived in this village for the last fifteen years. We are very happy and delighted that we choose this village to call our home. I was born and raised in this wonderful county and I am very proud to be a good old Norfolk boy. Let us now visit the place that we call home.

## Introduction to our Village

First let me introduce you to our village and then give you some insight into the village of Shouldham in the Past before taking you around the Shouldham of today. The Norfolk village of Shouldham is within easy reach of the beautiful North Norfolk coast. It is 8 miles south east of King's Lynn with Sandringham house just a few miles further on. Nearby are the villages of Marham, Shouldham Thorpe and South Runcton. The village of Shouldham lies about 7 miles north east of Downham Market. The village clusters around the attractive village green, home to the King's Arms public house recently re-opened as a community pub. Also close by is St. Martin at Shouldham school which is a Church of England primary academy and the other side of the green is the converted old school which is now called Chalk & Cheese that features a gift shop along with a bar, restaurant with bed and breakfast accommodation…

# My Village

## Introduction to our Village

Above we see the church, the green and Susie with Charlie and Poppy in our garden in 2014. All Saints' Church lies on the outskirts of the village in an elevated position looking out over the village itself in a beautiful setting. Built from a mixture of Carrstone and flint, the tower appears to be one of the earliest features, dating to the late 13th early 14th century. The splendid nave roof has alternating large and small hammer beams and features hammer posts bearing carved angels. Situated within the Nar Valley, Shouldham is in the lee of a chalk ridge that rises above the Fens to the west. Away from the village green on Westgate Street is the village post office then at the bottom of the road is Fairstead Drove that has the village Bowls Club and the village playground. Close by is the New Road where the Shouldham Retirement Home called Victoria Hall is located then heading back towards the village green on Eastgate Street you will find the Shouldham Village Hall. Past the playground and just outside the village is Shouldham Warren which features woodland walks, a Rhododendron avenue. Shouldham Warren is now managed under the same access rights as Thetford Forest that permits access and opportunities for public walking, cycling and horse riding. Shouldham today is a vibrant place to live and/or visit and has unlike many other small Norfolk villages and even towns managed to retain the small village feel and significantly many of its own resources. It still has its own church, school, post office, local bus service, care home, village green, village hall, playground, bowls club, King's Arms public house, Chalk and Cheese hostelry and of course the wonderful resource of Shouldham Warren close by. The parish also has a long history and was certainly well established by the time of the Norman Conquest, its population, land ownership and productive resources being extensively detailed in the Domesday Book of 1086. There is evidence of Iron Age settlement. In 1944 a rare sword was uncovered whilst digging for gravel near the village. Additionally, crop marks visible on aerial photographs taken over fields to the northeast of Shouldham village show two potential Iron Age roundhouses. So not only is Shouldham wonderful today but it also has a rich and varied history which we will now about to go and explore…

# My Village

## Shouldham of the Past

The parish of Shouldham is located in the west of Norfolk, within the Nar Valley. It lies to the east of the village of Marham, south of Wormegay and north of the village of Fincham. The name Shouldham derives from the Old English meaning 'homestead that paid rent'. The parish has a long history and was certainly well established by the time of the Norman Conquest, its population, land ownership and productive resources being extensively detailed in the Domesday Book of 1086. This book also reveals that before 1066 the lands were under the jurisdiction of the Thorkell's and that after the conquest Ralph Baynard took control of the area. The parish had lots of agricultural land and resources that included sheep as well as beehives, a mill and a fishery. Shouldham also had two churches at this time. The area around Shouldham was occupied from as early as the Mesolithic period of prehistory from 8000 to 2700 BC. Virtually every field on the southern slopes on the valley archaeologists have found worked Mesolithic and Neolithic flint tools. Five of these flint tools take the form of axe-heads but other tools like scrapers have also been found. It is also worth noting that an intriguing flint 'anvil stone' of prehistoric date was found at the highest point of Shouldham Warren. Shouldham and its surrounding area has been inhabited since the dawn of time since at least the Stone Age. Archaeologists field walking in the Shouldham area discovered two sites of particular interest amongst the numerous and widely distributed flint scatters. The first of these is located near to Shouldham Warren and constitutes a Mesolithic site that had been protected by peat deposits. This location was reused later during the Neolithic period for flint working, probably on a seasonal basis. The other site is situated atop a ridge in the valley. Interestingly archaeologists found several distinct pot boiler scatters on the site. Aerial photographs of Shouldham have revealed a number of enclosures which were visible as crop marks. Several of these took the form of ring ditches and it is possible that these indicate activity in the parish during the Bronze Age which was from 2700 to 1000 BC. The one located near to RAF Marham airfield has distinctly Bronze Age features. The discovery of Bronze Age cremation urns in the area of the later medieval priory (established in about 1190 AD for Gilbertine monks and nuns and was dissolved in 1538 AD) suggest Bronze Age occupation in the village of Shouldham during this period…

# My Village

## Shouldham of the Past

Whilst digging for gravel in a field near Shouldham in 1944 people found an Iron Age burial that contained an anthropoid sword which is an iron sword with a copper-alloy anthropoid handle. This sort of sword is a particularly rare find. Archaeology has recognised this sword as being one of international importance. Other Iron Age finds include some crop-marks visible on aerial photographs taken over fields to the northeast of Shouldham village that show crop-marks in the ground that could be of two Iron Age roundhouses. Whilst metal detecting around the village and the surrounding area people have uncovered seven Iron Age coins including several silver coins minted by the local Iceni tribe. This tribe is of significant importance not just to the history of the people of Norfolk but the UK and beyond. This is because Queen Boudica who was the local Norfolk chieftain Queen is famous for fighting and almost defeating the mighty Roman Army, way back in the first century AD. Her tribe the Iceni lived in what we now call Norfolk which is also the place of my birth. I am very proud that Boudica was a local girl (actually she was born in Wales and came to Norfolk as a young bride). She was married to King Prasutagus and upon his death her daughters were raped and she was flogged by the Romans. She then went on to fight the Romans until her death in AD 61. She is reputed to have had red hair and wore a blue dye called woad on her face to make her more frightening to her enemies. I am thrilled to think that all those years ago she may have passed through our village recruiting the local Iceni warriors to fight against the Romans. We may today be walking in her very footsteps! The village of Shouldham was also a centre of some importance during the Roman period (43 AD to 410 AD). Archaeologists have found that a large settlement existed in the village during this time and they have made a huge number of finds relating to domestic life, manufacturing, religion and ornamentation have been recovered from within the occupation area. Over 700 coins have been found in the village and their distribution may suggest some sort of ritual centre, a notion supported by the discovery of a votive staff on the site and a votive pal stave elsewhere in the parish. However, it is also possible that the sheer number of metalwork objects found means that this site was engaged in some sort of manufacturing and was thus an industrial centre. Perhaps this latter suggestion is more plausible as several pottery kiln sites and an iron-working site have also been found and recorded in the surrounding landscape…

# My Village

 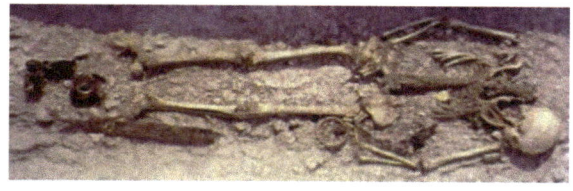

## Shouldham of the Past

A number of fine Roman artefacts have also been found at various locations in the village of Shouldham by metal detecting. A bracelet was found in Church Lane, a pendant in Gallow Lane, a seal box northwest of Mill Farm and a brooch on Shouldham Warren. As we leave the Roman period behind two Early Saxon inhumation cemeteries have been found and recorded in Shouldham. The fact that one of them overlies the Roman settlement site strongly suggests that it was in an important ceremonial position. The other cemetery was identified by the large number of brooches, pendants and dress fittings that were found. These items are good indicators of Saxon burials as individuals were often buried in their finest clothes and jewellery. A third much later cemetery, dating to the late Saxon early medieval period, has also been identified in Shouldham. This particular site was situated within a large pottery scatter, which may suggest that a settlement was located here during the end of the Saxon period. Several other Saxon small finds have been found in Shouldham including a magnificent gold sword belt mount, a pendant made from a pierced 4th century Roman coin and a cruciform brooch. Shouldham appears to have been an attractive location for contemplation and worship during the medieval period. A Gilbertine Priory was built to the northeast of the modern village in about 1190 to house a community of monks and nuns. It was dissolved in 1538 and the ruins were removed in part during 1840. The present Abbey Farm house sits over the nave of the Priory church. Many earthworks belonging to the Priory lie to the south of the farm building and these consist of quite complex water channels, rectangular enclosures and fishponds. The most striking feature of the Priory is the central north-south channel that neatly divides the site into two roughly equal portions for reasons unknown. A great variety of finds have been recovered from the Priory including medieval stone coffins and medieval page turners. A number of the buildings on Westgate Street also incorporate blocks of medieval stone. As these buildings date to the 19th century it is possible that these blocks came from the Priory as it was pulled down during this period. At this time the parish also had two fully operational churches: St Margaret's and All Saints', both of which were mentioned in the Domesday Book. St Margaret's was still standing in 1519 but fell from use at some time thereafter. In 1840 its ruins were rediscovered after lowering a hill in a field adjoining the All Saints' Church. Nothing much now remains but various flints and medieval bricks can be seen on a slightly raised ground surface…

# My Village

Our dogs
Charlie and Poppy
In 2020

## Shouldham of the Past

The village surviving All Saints' Church is built from a mixture of carstone and flint. The tower is one of the earliest features, dating to the late 13th early 14th century. The modern appearance of the nave owes much to a restoration in 1870 fortunately this work left the splendid 15th century nave roof intact. This special roof has alternating large and small hammer beams and features hammer posts bearing carved angels. The actual settlement of Shouldham, in medieval times, lay behind Colt's Hall to the east of the modern village. This deserted medieval settlement was discovered in 1970. Investigation of the site in 1974 and 1983 showed very fine earthworks relating to building platforms, enclosures, tofts and a hollow way that ran east to west between the church and Colts Hall. The earthworks were fortunately underneath untouched pastureland and survived in good condition. However, since 2001 they have been subject to a protection agreement to ensure their continued survival. According to the Ordnance Survey, Shouldham had a livestock market twice annually during the medieval period. The site of this 'Fair Stead Market' has been placed northwest of the village in the plantation of the same name…

# My Village

## Shouldham of the Past

There was a full time market operating in the village by 1334 and because of this the village was referred to as Shouldham Market at that time. To prove this field walking and metal detecting found numerous sherds of pottery, several pieces of metalwork which included items such as coins, buckles and strap ends. In the post medieval period the hilly and windswept landscape of Shouldham was exploited for corn milling. 18th and 19th century maps show two windmills in the parish and a kiln for lime burning. An early 19th century map also shows a pottery/brick kiln in Shouldham. The manufacture of bricks and the production of flour would have helped to supplement the income that the villagers made from farming. Several of Shouldham's finer buildings were built during the post medieval period and have been listed as properties of architectural interest. The most impressive of these is Colt's Hall, which dates to around 1830. Another house of note is The Spar, which is set facing the village green and comprised of a house with a shop front that dates to around 1760. It also has 20th century alterations including the plate glass shop front. However, perhaps the most interesting structure erected in the post medieval period was a freestone obelisk that was used as a drinking fountain. It was still in existence in 1839 but sadly it has since disappeared from sight. The most recent archaeological record for Shouldham relates to World War One and World War Two military sites. The RAF base at Marham extends into Shouldham parish. The Royal Flying Corps first used this airfield during World War One. The Royal Air Force took over the site during World War Two. In 1980 Cold War Hardened Nuclear Shelters were built here and are considered to be of national importance. In 1979 the huge set of earthworks and collection of ruined buildings in Shouldham Warren were investigated. The judgement was that the earthworks and buildings in the Warren probably date to World War Two, and may be the remnants of a shooting range or temporary camp. Having explored the villages past we will now enter the village of Shouldham as it is today…

# My Village

## The Shouldham of Today

The village of Shouldham is a very pleasant village to live in, laying in a hollow and when approached from the West, with the sun shining from that direction too, you overlook most of the village with the Church on the hill to the East and some of the trees of Shouldham Forest showing up on the left hand side as you commence your descent into the village. Anyone with a liking for scenery will have to admit to seeing one of the prettiest sights in the district. The village appears to have got its name from a small rivulet of water which flows through the village and empties itself into the Sandy Drain near Mere Plot farm which is on the edge of the Shouldham Warren. The early Saxon name for such a stream is Scole, Scult, Scoult and Shoud. If you add ham for home on the end of Shoud we get Shoudham and then more recently we get Shouldham. The village of Shouldham is built around the small village green and the surrounding village roads. It is 5½ miles North East of Downham Market, and 10 miles West of Swaffham. The village of Shouldham benefits from having a local bus service that runs between Marham, Shouldham and Kings Lynn. The bus provides a vital lifeline for many villagers. The village green has a phone box and post box as well as a flag pole and seating for weary travellers. It is also the venue for the village summer fate were villages can meet and have fun. The village pub provides a welcome beer tent, refreshments are also available and local school children enjoy all the fun of the summer fate whilst local dog owners enter their pride and joy into the annual dog show which is also held on the green. At the same time as the summer fate other members of the community hold yard sales at their properties all around the village. Susie and I have often held a yard sale at our property and as well as making a few pounds selling items we have had a great time meeting all the villagers and visitors alike. Some people in the village also produce a regular news letter to keep their fellow residents informed of up and coming events being held in and around the village. These can include such events as barn dinner dances, Christmas events, flower shows, coffee mornings etc. Local residence also sell their own produce by the roadside such as fruit, vegetables, plants, honey and fresh eggs. There is a lot going on in the village and many of these events take place in or around the following village venues…

# My Village

Ginny, Susie, Charlie
and Poppy
In
Shouldham Warren

## The Shouldham of Today

The parish church, (All Saints,) is at the east end of the village. It contains a handsome marble monument, bearing a finely executed figure of Faith. On the wall of the cemetery are several large gravestones, one of which has interestingly the insignia of a Knight Templar. There can be few more lovely spots in the village than this churchyard overlooking the village in the valley below. The First World War memorial stands like a sentinel, and in the field beneath there are medieval earthworks which stretch away towards the village. Shown above is St. Martin at Shouldham school which is a Church of England primary academy and it is graded as **OUTSTANDING** by Ofsted. The school opened in September 2000, following the amalgamation of the village primary schools at Fincham and Shouldham. In 2014 it became a member of the Dioceses of Ely Multi-Academy Trust. The school is in a small village setting and has close links with the local community. It caters for around 240 children from rising 3 years to 11 years of age. It is a feeder school to Downham Market High School. The school serves the immediate parishes of Shouldham, Fincham and Shouldham Thorpe, but children also travel from other nearby villages and towns. In September 2005 a Nursery was added, which now caters for 26 pupils in a purpose built classroom and outdoor area. It has a fantastic, modern building, with top class eco-credentials. There are eight classrooms, a library/ Eco-Lab, large hall, kitchen and office suite. The schools extensive outside space includes a large playground, playing fields, a bandstand, landscaped quiet areas, trim trail and a wild forest area. The school has installed geothermal heating, rainwater harvesting, solar powered water heating and a wind turbine in recent years. The school fosters good relationships with the local villagers and holds various events through-out the year including sports days, out of term time activities for the children and they hold a very successful Christmas fair every year in the school hall…

# My Village

## The Shouldham of Today

Pictured above is the King's Arms public house in the village of Shouldham which has been in existence for centuries. It was voted Camra pub of the year in West Norfolk for the last three years (2017 to 2019). Today it serves the community that rescued it from oblivion and provides award winning pub grub. The pub is set on Shouldham's beautiful village green, the King's Arms is a traditional 17th-century hostelry proud of its locality. Here you'll find real ales served straight from the cask; good-value food using fresh local produce from Norfolk's bountiful larder; a large, child-friendly garden; public bars, a cafe and a friendly atmosphere where everyone both young and old, families and friends, diners and drinkers are all welcomed with a friendly smile. Across the village green from the pub is the building that now houses Chalk and Cheese guest house. It is a converted Victorian primary school house. It has a dining area, hall, bar, lounge, bedrooms for hire, a small gift shop, garden and other garden buildings. The original school building was erected in 1866 and was all at one level. Some of the original dividers from the main double classroom can now be seen as part of the divider between the hall and the kitchen. In the building at the bottom of the stairs is a collage of pictures taken when it was a functioning school and above the snug fireplace is an original carved inscription. The old school looks over the village green and the community owned pub. Opposite and to the left of the old school there is a field that can be walked through that takes you up towards the Church of All Saints. The field is designated as a historic monument as it was the location of the original village of Shouldham in Saxon times before it was obliterated after the outbreak of the "black death"…

# My Village

## The Shouldham of Today

The Shouldham Village Hall, situated in Eastgate Street has a large hall (capacity 100 persons) and a smaller annexe. In recent years the kitchens in the hall have been modernised to such an extent that the village hall now provides the school with pupil dinners for St. Martin at Shouldham. The large hall is regularly used for village children's birthday parties, social and fund-raising events, exercise classes and meetings. The annexe is more suitable for holding small meetings in. The hall has a separate kitchen, toilets, car parking and a ramp for disabled access. In Shouldham we have been very fortunate to have had a functioning post office service located on Westgate Street however, in March 2019 it had to close. I am pleased to report that the post office re-opened in October 2019. It is providing the villagers with a full postal service into 2020. The Shouldham Post Office is open Monday-Friday during the week, on weekends they are open Saturday mornings. The Shouldham Bowls Club and the village Playing Field are just off the bottom of Westgate Street on Fairstead Drove. The bowls clubs address is The New Clubhouse, Fairstead Drove, Shouldham, Kings Lynn PE33 0DL. The club was formed in 1946. It is interesting to note that the wearing of shorts by members and guests is permitted by the club. The club should be contacted if you wish to find out more information regarding the facilities provided. Situated close by is the Shouldham King George Playing Field which offers a safe young children's play area as well as grass sports pitches. There is space for 30 cars to park in a designated area. There are changing facilities on site, a disabled toilet and the park is open to the public from dawn to dusk every day…

# My Village

Susie, Ginny, Charlie Poppy and the cycle club at Christmas time in the Warren

## The Shouldham of Today

The Shouldham Retirement Home Victoria Hall is a privately owned Care Home that only provides residential care and is registered for a maximum of 37 service users in the following needs areas: Dementia, Old Age, Physical Disability and Sensory Impairment. They also provide specialist care for suffers of: Alzheimer's, Cancer Care, Colitis & Crohn's Disease, Huntington's Disease, Multiple Sclerosis, Orthopaedic, Parkinson's Disease, Speech Impairment, Stroke and Visual Impairment for ages 65+. Some of the staff speak (other than English): Hindi and Polish. The care home has 37 single rooms with 12 having en suite facilities. The home provides the following facilities and Services: Day Care, Respite Care and Convalescent Care. They also have their own separate Dementia Care Unit, their own GP if required and they can provide furniture if required. Pets are permitted by arrangement. The home has wheelchair access and provides ground floor accommodation only. There are gardens for the residents to enjoy. All rooms have a phone and TV point. Just outside the village is the wonderful Shouldham Warren. Susie and I have two lovely dogs called Poppy and Charlie and the last village facility is by far our personal favourite place to go. The Shouldham Warren which is administered by the Forestry Commission provides not just a wild life haven but also some well-maintained walking and cycling paths. At the Warren we have the opportunity to observe the woodland itself, the wild life it supports and enjoy some wide ranging views out over the surrounding landscape. At the Warren all paths initially head away from the car park. Most stay within the confines of the Warren but a longer walk also visits Wormegay and passes near to two churches, both unfortunately kept locked due to their remote positions. Wormegay Castle, close by, originally was an Anglo-Saxon manor but was converted into a motte-and-bailey castle in the 12th century. Today all that remains there is an encompassing rampart, ditch and an extensive bailey and a building platform. All signposted walks finish on paths within the Warren. In 2020 the Warren is under threat by developers who want to destroy the trees, stop public access, and dig a quarry for extraction of silicon sand. This will not only be an environmental disaster but stop local people and the wider community from enjoying the natural environment that the Warren gives us! I hope this fails as Susie and I like many other villagers visit the Warren daily with our dogs Poppy and Charlie who really enjoy this wonderful place. Talking about dogs in the next chapter you will need to take your binoculars with you as we discovering the wildlife of Norfolk…

# Norfolk Wildlife

As you know I was born and raised in this wonderful county and I am very proud to be an old Norfolk boy. One of the things that I love about this county is its rich and diverse wildlife. In Norfolk we have, amongst other wildlife, seals, fish and shell fish in our coastal waters whilst in the air we have magnificent sea birds, birds of prey, song birds and many more birds that you will see in the fields and the gardens of Norfolk, such as wrens, blackbirds and of course the robin. Land based wildlife is also plentiful in the Norfolk fields, woods, farm land, hedgerows, parks and our gardens. You may well be lucky enough to see such delights as foxes, badgers and hares for example. If like us, you live in the county many of these also venture into our country gardens. To celebrate our myriad of great wildlife we have in Norfolk I have featured examples of most of the wildlife that can be seen in Norfolk in the pages that follow. You may however, see other wildlife, not mentioned, as you venture around Norfolk, that is the joy of being in the beautiful Norfolk landscape and seeing, for yourself, the wonderful wildlife that is all around you. So with your binoculars in hand lets discover the wonderful Wildlife of Norfolk…

# Norfolk Wildlife

## Adder

**The Adder** is Britain's most widespread reptile and our only venomous snake. It can be found throughout Norfolk, in a variety of open and man-made habitats. Although they have suffered somewhat from the reduction of moorland habitat in Norfolk, they remain relatively widespread. We live and exercise our two dogs in Shouldham Warren and have seen several Adder's whilst walking through the woods. Like most snakes, the adder can survive a fairly long time without eating, particularly in cooler weather and when hibernating over the winter months. It hunts by approaching slowly towards its prey and then it strikes, biting and quickly releasing its prey. Its victim will then succumb to the snakes venom within three minutes and will then be swallowed whole. The prey of the Adder are mainly frogs, newts, lizards, small mammals and birds eggs. Despite their venomous bite, adders will always attempt to flee from danger rather than confront it and its bite is rarely fatal for humans. Their main natural predators include buzzards and herons.

## Badger

**The Badger** is the largest member of the Mustelid family and Norfolk's largest land carnivore. They are nocturnal, emerging at dusk in summer to spend the night foraging. In winter they are much less active but they do not hibernate. They live in social groups of four to twelve adults and when they are not active they lie up in an extensive system of underground tunnels and nesting chambers known as setts. The female is called the sow, the male the boar. Badgers are now protected by a number of laws. The Protection of Badgers Act 1992 consolidated past legislation, which had made badger baiting and digging illegal and in addition made it an offence to damage, destroy or obstruct their setts. This protection has enabled the UK badger population to dramatically increase to the point where it is said to equal that of the red fox in some areas…

# Norfolk Wildlife

## Bank Vole, Field Vole and Water Vole

**The Bank Vole** is a common small rodent found in the Norfolk woodland, scrub and hedgerows. It is not quite as common in the more open Norfolk countryside as the vole. Bank voles are good climbers and will often use the disused nest of a hedgerow bird as its larder. They are highly vocal, often squeaking and chattering, sometimes using sounds too high in pitch to be detected by human ears. The predators of the Bank Vole include owls, kestrels, weasels and foxes. **The Field Vole** are one of the two most common small rodents of the countryside, found throughout Norfolk. Field vole differs from the bank vole by having shaggy, grey-brown fur and a very short and pinker tail than other vole species. Their food is primarily succulent grass stems, but roots, bulbs and bark, particularly in winter when fresh vegetation is much harder to find. Sometimes huge numbers of field vole's build up, but none survive for more than one winter. **The Water Vole** sadly is now the most endangered mammal species in the UK. Nearly 90% have disappeared in the last few years, mainly due to habitat loss. The water vole is found throughout Norfolk, though their distribution is patchy. Being semi-aquatic, it has flaps of skin over the ears to keep the water out when swimming. The water vole's burrows usually have entrances above and below the water. The predators of the water voles are mink, otters, stoats, weasels, brown rats, domestic cats, pike, herons and barn owls…

# Norfolk Wildlife

## Barn Owl

**The Barn Owl** is one of the world's most widespread birds. It can be found throughout Africa, India, the Far East, Australia, USA, the Caribbean, South America and Europe, where Britain is the northern most tip of its range. In Norfolk, which is a mainly agricultural county, we have many barns that provide a home for these wonderful creatures. Currently the Norfolk population of Barn Owls is in decline due to loss of habitat and prey species. Norfolk is however, ideal for Barn owls as they prefer to live in open country with some trees for cover and nesting sites. They usually become active at dusk, when they can be seen flying low over the ground in a slow, wavering flight with occasional short glides. The barn owl is an expert hunter with excellent vision and hearing that enables it to pinpoint its prey in near total darkness. It flies low, slowly, silently and swoops to the ground at the last moment to grasp its prey with its sharp claws. Small rodents make up most of its diet. They are swallowed whole and later any indigestible parts are regurgitated in the form of pellets. Barn owls do not hoot, but both young and adults make snoring and shrieking noises when at the nest…

# Norfolk Wildlife

## Little Owl and Tawny Owl

**The Little Owl** is the most commonly seen owl in Norfolk. It is Britain's smallest resident owl and easily identified by its compact shape and staring yellow eyes. Its favoured habitat is farmland and it is often seen at dusk or even in the daytime, sitting on a post or telegraph pole next to a Norfolk road or lane. Little owls hunt from perches such as these, pouncing on small mammals, birds and insects, particularly earthworms and beetles. Their call is a whistling sound, not unlike a lapwing or a mewing cat. In flight they can be seen usually low to the ground following a gently undulating path. **The Tawny Owl** is found extensively in Norfolk. It is totally nocturnal, roosting by day in a hollow tree or thick bush, often holly. Its habitat is very different to the barn owl, being mainly woodland areas and its diet of small mammals and birds will also consist of more woodland species such as mice. Its nest will generally be in a tree and is constructed of wood-dust, pellets and feathers or material scavenged from other bird's nests…

# Norfolk Wildlife

## Grass Snake and Buzzard

**The Grass Snake** is the largest reptile in Britain, growing to about one metre long. Its preferred habitat is damp areas like ponds, reservoirs and marshes, also making use of the surrounding terrestrial habitat such as grassland, scrub and woodland. We have some in our local Shouldham Warren. They feed mostly on amphibians and small fish. If threatened, they may lie still, pretending to be dead, but can rear up in mock attack, hissing. They also excrete a foul-smelling substance, particularly if handled, but are otherwise they are completely harmless. The females mate at most every other year, but can live to 25 years of age. Unlike the other native British snakes, they lay eggs and incubate them until they hatch in late summer. In warm weather they can be seen basking in the sun. Like all snakes, they are cold-blooded and can only be active and hunt when they raise their body temperature in this way. **The Buzzard** is the UK's most common large bird of prey, found mainly in the western half of the country but recently they have spread into Norfolk in great numbers. They live in all types of habitat from open farmland to uplands with wooded valleys. Frequently seen soaring in groups high in the sky on hot air thermals while emitting a distinctive mewing cry, they have keen eyesight, eight times better than humans. They usually hunt from low perches such as gate posts and fences, feeding mainly on small mammals and other animals. Susie and I often see them, while sitting in our Norfolk garden, being mobbed by gulls and/or crows who see them as a competitor for their food…

# Norfolk Wildlife

## Red Fox

**The Red Fox** is a remarkably adaptable and successful animal found in Norfolk, wherever food is plentiful and in almost every kind of habitat. The fox has been successful because it is willing to eat almost anything and has become particularly adept at surviving alongside man in farmland and urban areas alike. The fox with its bushy tail, large ears and narrow muzzle is unmistakable. The coat colour can be extremely variable. It is usually reddish-brown on top with lighter undersides, but much darker or even silvery forms are not uncommon. The mating season of the fox is December to February when the vixen can be heard at night uttering its eerie, high pitched scream. Four or five cubs are usually born in the spring and the female fox stays with them in the earth for two weeks, fed by the dog fox. The cubs remain with their mother until autumn when they disperse to find territories and mates of their own. The life expectancy of the fox is very short; 12 - 18 months in urban areas, (58% of all foxes are sadly killed on the roads of Norfolk by cars and lorries every year) and live very rarely beyond 3 years of age in rural areas…

# Norfolk Wildlife

## Brown Rat and Our Dogs Poppy and Charlie

**The Brown Rat** is a widespread pest, highly adaptable, a great opportunist and will live anywhere, wherever food and shelter are available. If you live in a Norfolk village, town or city, you are probably never more than 15 metres from a rat. Twenty percent of the world's food supply is either destroyed or eaten by rats. Brown rats arrived in the UK in 1730 from the Baltic, having originated in China and soon displaced the Black Rat by eating their young. They multiply at an alarming rate and live in large colonies. If left unchecked these colonies could number hundreds, despite a very high mortality rate. Brown rats are mainly nocturnal and are good swimmers. They will run away from danger, but may attack in groups if cornered. Packs of rats have been known to attack rabbits, large birds or even fish. They identify each other by smell and will fight off rival packs or even members of their own family if provoked. Their main predators are cats, dogs, owls and weasels and of course man. Our two dogs Poppy and Charlie are very good at catching rats…

# Norfolk Wildlife

## Fallow Deer and Muntjac Deer

**The Fallow Deer** were first thought to have been brought to England by the Romans, but the main introduction was made by the Normans in the eleventh century for ornamental and hunting purposes. Fallow Deer are very docile, non-territorial, herding deer that thrives in parklands, making it ideal for semi-domestication. The current patchy distribution of the Fallow Deer reflects the distribution of ancient deer parks and hunting forests. Feral deer (escapees from parks) are now common in Norfolk. Herds may number a hundred if conditions are right. There are now more deer in Norfolk today than there were 500 years ago in the reign of Queen Elizabeth I. Fallow Deer have palmate (palm-like) antlers with a wider and flatter spread with less distinct tines than the red deer. **The Muntjac Deer** was introduced into Britain from China in 1900, many later escaped from the private estates they lived on and are now well established in Norfolk and the rest of the UK, where they colonize woodland and dense scrub land. Active by day or night muntjac are mostly seen at dusk. They utter loud barks over prolonged periods and equally loud distress calls. We often hear them when we are in our garden in the evening. They are mainly solitary animals but may be seen in family groups. The males, or bucks, have short backward curving antlers which are shed in May or June and re-grow to full size by October or November. These are not used as weapons, but instead the elongated, protruding tusk-like teeth of the male can be used for this purpose. In common with all deer species except the reindeer, the female does not have antlers or the elongated teeth of the male...

# Norfolk Wildlife

## Red Deer and Roe Deer

**The Red Deer** are Norfolk and Britain's largest native land mammal and, together with the roe deer, are our only native deer species. All other deer species have been introduced. In all deer species (except the reindeer) only the male has antlers. Antlers are shed each spring and immediately a new set starts to grow, taking 16 weeks to reach full size in August. They are made of a type of dense and very solid bone and whilst growing are covered with a hairy skin called velvet which is shed when the antlers have reached their full size for that year. The stag uses his antlers to fight other males during the mating season, known as the rut, which lasts for three weeks in October. **The Roe Deer** are one of only two native species of deer in Britain and the most widespread today. They are rare in Wales and absent from eastern Kent and parts of the Midlands, but in southern England and Norfolk they are increasing in numbers. They are active day and night, browsing in mostly woodland areas but may also be spotted in larger gardens in rural or suburban areas. Roe deer are fiercely territorial and the males, or bucks, will aggressively defend their territory, especially through the summer. Threats in the wild are few, as their natural predators, the wolf and the lynx, are now extinct in Britain. Young fawns may fall prey to foxes or eagles, but most casualties are from road traffic or farm machinery. Many young fawns will not survive the cold of their first winter, but those that do may live up to ten years of age in the wild…

# Norfolk Wildlife

**Grey Squirrel and Hedgehog**

**The Grey Squirrel** was introduced into this country from North America between 1876 and 1910. Within 100 years they had completely replaced the native red squirrel in Norfolk and all but the northern-most parts of the country. This was mainly because of their ability to utilize more of the available foods found in broad leaved deciduous woodland, and also their transmission of a deadly virus. Grey squirrels eat buds and shoots, nuts, seeds and fungi. Their sharp incisor teeth can very quickly cut a hole in any nut shell which they hold in their forefeet. They then crack it open in a crowbar-like action to extract the kernel inside. They are popular with the public, people often put food out for them, especially in urban areas where they are among the most visible wild mammals in the garden. We have regular visits from them to our garden. **The Hedgehog** is plentiful in Norfolk and are native to mainland Britain. The hedgehog has a powerful forefoot and claws for digging for its favourite food of slugs and worms. They may eat forty or more slugs in a night. Hedgehogs can also climb, swim and can sprint a surprisingly fast 6 mph! If threatened they can roll up into a ball as protection against predators. Their biggest enemy apart from humans is the badger. Hedgehogs hibernate alone from November to April under a supporting structure such as a shed, wood piles, brambles or bonfire heaps. They may, however, emerge to forage at night during any milder winter spells. We often see them in our garden in the early summer evenings…

# Norfolk Wildlife

## Harvest Mouse, House Mouse and Wood Mouse

**The Harvest Mouse** is the smallest rodent in Norfolk, weighing just six grams. The harvest mouse has a truly prehensile tail that can be used as a fifth limb. When wrapped around a stem it can act as a brake or anchor. This makes it very nimble travelling and feeding in stems of cereals and grasses. They have a remarkable ability to sense vibrations through the soles of their feet. **The House Mouse** lives close to man in gardens, farm buildings, houses and factory sites. Further afield they can be found wherever food is plentiful with cereals, bread and fats being their main foods. Their incisor teeth have open roots, allowing them to keep growing throughout their life. They have a razor sharp front edge and are also self-sharpening, so that they can gnaw through even the hardest materials. They can jump high and climb vertical wooden surfaces. In buildings and houses they can be a pest as they frequently gnaw through plastic and electrical cables. **The Wood Mouse** is also known as the long-tailed field mouse, this is the most common mouse in our Norfolk countryside, found in woods, scrub and hedgerows. The wood mouse is mainly nocturnal. It will sit up and wash all over, especially if scared. It is an excellent climber and will leap high in the air when disturbed. It has many enemies; weasels, stoats, cats, foxes, moles and owls. It has a varied diet, eating nuts, seeds, rose hips, small insects and larvae…

# Norfolk Wildlife

## Kestrel

**The Kestrel** is one of Norfolk's most common bird of prey, easily identified hovering low over the ground searching for food. It hovers by flying into a light headwind, making continuous adjustments of its wings and tail while it hangs on a rising draught of air. This allows it to keep its head perfectly still and spot the slightest movement on the ground below. When prey is in sight, it drops vertically to the ground, grabs it in its talons and killing it with a swift bite. Prey is mostly small mammals such as voles, but kestrels are adaptable and will switch to beetles, earthworms or even snails. They frequently use pylons or telegraph poles as vantage points to spot prey, saving themselves the effort of hovering. In winter many more kestrels visit Norfolk from the Netherlands and Scandinavia...

# Norfolk Wildlife

# Mink and Mole

**The Mink** is a medium-sized member of the weasel family. The first American mink were brought to British fur farms in 1929 and all wild mink in Norfolk and the UK today are descendants of escapees. The natural wild colouring of the mink in the USA is a glossy dark brown, appearing almost black in some light. Commercial farming selectively bred much paler colours, hence most of those in the wild in Norfolk are a lighter brown. Mink spend up to 80% of their time in their dens, sleeping, grooming and eating food that they have carried back to their den. Mink are frequently found near water, they are often mistaken for otters, although mink are in fact considerably smaller. Mink are a major factor in the reduction of the water vole population in Norfolk, because they are small enough to follow their prey down its burrow. However, recent research indicates that where the otter population has increased, due to cleaner rivers, mink have declined. **The Mole** is common throughout Norfolk and the UK, but are rarely seen as they spend almost their entire time underground, only occasionally appearing above ground at the top of one of their characteristic molehills, and even then usually only the head and pink fleshy snout is revealed. Moles have a well-developed sense of orientation retaining a mental plan of their complex layout of underground tunnels. The uniform texture of the fur allows it to lie in any direction, making it easier for the animal to reverse rapidly in their tunnels. When the soil is shallow or subject to flooding, large molehills known as 'fortresses' may be formed. They can be up to a metre high and contain a nest chamber and several radial tunnels. The tail is carried erect and it is probable that the hairs on the tip give the mole information about its surroundings by brushing against the tunnel roof…

# Norfolk Wildlife

## Otter and Rabbit

**The Otter** is a large member of the weasel family (mustelids) with an amphibious lifestyle. In the wild, in Norfolk, they are elusive, secretive animals living in undisturbed rivers, streams and estuaries. In the early 1960's they were on the verge of extinction due to river pollution, habitat loss and hunting. Now with full legal protection, cleaner rivers and managed habitat the otter is returning to its former haunts, though its distribution will always be limited by the availability of fish. The male otter is called a dog and the female a bitch. They have large lungs and can stay submerged under water for 4 minutes, often swimming 400 metres before resurfacing. They can reach speeds of 12 km/h under water and can easily outrun humans on land. The males occupy large ranges, which may include up to 20 km of river bank and daily travel long distances along regular routes by the margins of the river. **The Rabbit** was originally from Spain and south-west France, the rabbit was brought to England in the 12th century by the Normans and kept in captivity in warrens as a source of meat and fur. Close to where we live is Shouldham Warren. The name could well have originated from being used to raise rabbits in the past. Many escaped into the wild and eventually become so common that farming them was no longer economic. Helped by fast breeding, a diet of virtually any vegetable matter and despite persecution by predators, the rabbit slowly established itself in the wild in Norfolk, despite originally favouring a warmer, drier climate. In the 1950's, the disease myxomatosis was introduced to curb their numbers and the rabbit almost became extinct, but is once again a common animal of the countryside. It can however, be a serious pest for farmers, eating and damaging crops. The male is called a buck and the female a doe. The main predators of rabbits are the stoat and the fox, although young animals are also taken by birds of prey and weasels…

# Norfolk Wildlife

## Stoat and Weasel

**The Stoat** is a member of the weasel family (Mustelids), stoats are found throughout Norfolk and mainland Britain in a variety of habitats. Their appearance is similar to the weasel, although the stoat is considerably larger and has a distinctive black tip to its tail. Stoats are very agile, they can climb well and may take young birds in the nest. They are also strong swimmers, capable of crossing large rivers. Their primary food source is the rabbit, despite being many times its own weight, supplemented with small rodents and birds. The number of stoats in the wild is usually linked to the rabbit population but in recent years their numbers have declined. Like the weasel, they are still heavily persecuted by Norfolk gamekeepers protecting their game birds, but the numbers shot in recent years have also reduced, so it is more likely that they are being affected through eating poisoned rats or mice. **The Weasel** is the smallest member of the Mustelid family and Norfolk's smallest carnivore. It is smaller than the stoat and has no black tip to its tail, although it does have small white patches under its chin and throat. Like the stoat it is still persecuted by many gamekeepers. The weasel may travel up to 2.5 km on a hunting expedition. It climbs well and will often raid bird's nests, taking the eggs and young. Female weasels are considerably smaller than males, but both are small enough to pursue rats, mice and even field voles into their own tunnels. The weasel is common in most habitats and is very active both day and night as it must consume a quarter to a third of its body weight every day to survive.

With our binoculars in hand we will now focus in on the wildlife that can often be seen by visitors to the world famous wetlands of the Norfolk Broads…

# Norfolk Wildlife

## Wildlife on the Norfolk Broads

In Norfolk locals often refer to the area of the Norfolk Broads as "The Broadland", as some of the rivers and broads make their way into neighbouring Suffolk and/or the North Sea. The wildlife abounds in the landscape, adapting to the ever changing environment. Conservation has been very successful in reintroducing species such as some of those mentioned in this section.

**Chinese Water Deer** - Introduced from China in the nineteenth century, the Chinese water deer stands at only 50-55 cm high and has large rounded ears and a cute face. Males do not have antlers but instead their canine teeth grow downwards to form two tusks that they use for fighting.

**Otter** – Otters are agile, playful and surprisingly large reaching 95-30 cm in length, otters have a distinctive white throat and can often be found in the quiet back waters of the Norfolk Broads.

**Water Vole** - Generally dark brown, these squat furry rodents have blunt noses, inconspicuous ears and a hair covered tail. They live in slow flowing water, water voles are often found in dykes and streams with soft earth banks that run into the Norfolk broads.

**Bittern** - With their distinctive booming call the elusive bittern are more often heard than seen. Extremely well camouflaged they can usually be found in the reed beds of the Norfolk Broads.

**Cetti's Warbler** - With its deceptively loud birdsong you would imagine the Cetti's warbler would be easy to spot. Sadly this is not the case. These secretive birds tend to hide in the dense reed beds of the Norfolk Broads.

**Common Tern** - These slender gull like birds have a long association with the Norfolk Broads, easy to spot with their silver grey plumage, black cap, red beak and legs…

# Norfolk Wildlife

## Wildlife on the Norfolk Broads

**Great Crested Grebe** – They are easy to spot during the summer with their distinctive breeding plumage, great crested grebes sit low in the water with a long neck and sharp beak. They have chestnut cheeks, white eyes and a black crest.

**Kingfisher** - Notoriously difficult to spot, the Kingfisher's bright blue colouring makes them one of the UK's most striking birds. You will often only hear their piercing call and not see them.

**Marsh Harrier** - Regularly seen flying low over the marshes of the Norfolk Broads this spectacular bird of prey is the largest of the harriers and males have distinctive black wing tips.

**Reed Warbler** - The reed warbler can be found in the reed beds of the Norfolk Broads. Well camouflaged, it builds its basket shaped nest around the reed stems.

**Siskin** - This active yellow bird has a forked tail and a distinctive yellow stripe on its forked wings. A common sight on the Broads.

**Common Blue Damselfly** - Only the male of the species is actually blue. His colour is distinguishable in its vividness compared to other blue damselfly species and he has a strong blob of blue towards the tip of his tail. The female is a far less impressive brown colour. They are often found flying low over water on the surface and in the reed beds on the Broads.

**Norfolk Hawker Dragonfly** - This endangered species has clear wings, green eyes and a distinctive yellow triangle shape on its body. The Norfolk Hawker dragonfly thrives in the ditches of un-spoilt grazing marshes close to the Norfolk Broads.

**Swallowtail Butterfly** - These distinctive butterflies are exclusive to the Norfolk Broads and their 9 cm wingspan make them the largest native British butterfly. Look out for their yellow and black wings and forked tail. They are a joy to see when on the Broads.

Still grasping your binoculars in hand and having spent some time on the Norfolk Broads we now venture onto dry land and head for the Norfolk Coast to see what other wonderful Norfolk wildlife awaits us by the seaside…

# Norfolk Wildlife

## Coastal Wildlife in Norfolk

On the Norfolk coast the sandy beaches and stunning coastline with its salt water of the North Sea supports colonies of grey and common seals that thrive. The sea off the Norfolk coast is a rich environment for sea life and provide a protein high source of food for not just sea birds but for humans as well. Our local sea has such fish in it as cod, haddock, pollock, herring, skate and mackerel and many more. Shellfish are also found around the Norfolk coast. These include such beautiful shellfish as crabs, lobsters, mussels, oysters, scallops, whelks, shrimps and cockles which are all popular types of edible shellfish. All of which makes the coast of Norfolk a must visit location for summer visitors. Local dog walkers, us included, use the beaches the whole year round. There is nothing more bracing or beautiful than a walk on a Norfolk beach on Christmas Day or Boxing Day watching the sea birds swoop over the sea. We will at first focus on the Sea Birds swooping just off the Norfolk coast…

# Norfolk Wildlife

## Norfolk Coastal Sea Birds

We will now meet the sea birds that live and thrive over, on and sometimes under the seawater off the Norfolk coast.

**Grebes** - Grebes are diving water birds, feeding on small fish and aquatic invertebrates. The Little Grebe or 'Dabchick', is the UK's smallest grebe, about half the size of a Moorhen. Grebes nest on floating platforms made up of waterweed.

**Arctic Tern** - The Arctic Tern is a medium-sized tern, which nests in colonies on sand and shingle beaches along the Norfolk coast. Arctic Terns are noisy in their colonies and, like most terns, will attack intruders threatening their young, often dive-bombing them with their sharp bills at the ready.

**Kittiwake** - The Kittiwake is our most sea-loving gull, only turning up inland on odd occasions and spending winter out on the Atlantic. A medium-sized, elegant and gentle-looking gull, it eats fish, shrimps and worms, and does not scavenge at landfill sites like other gulls. It nests in colonies on cliff tops and rock ledges from February until August.

**Herring Gull** - The Herring Gull (see above) is a familiar sight in our seaside towns, particularly during the breeding season. In winter it can be found on farmland, wetland and coastal habitats, inland landfill sites, playing fields, and reservoirs. The distinctive red spot on its bill is used by the chicks who will peck at any long, yellow thing with a red spot in order to get food.

**Black Headed Gull** - The Black-headed Gull is a familiar sight on farmland, wetland and coastal habitats throughout Norfolk. It nests on salt marshes and on islands in flooded gravel pits and reservoirs, and sometimes forms very large, noisy colonies. There are about 140,000 breeding pairs in the UK and up to 2.2 million wintering birds arrive each year…

# Norfolk Wildlife

## Norfolk Coastal Sea Birds

**Razorbill** - The Razorbill is a medium-sized auk that nests on ledges and amongst rocks at the bottom of cliffs. It feeds on fish which it catches by diving from the surface and swimming underwater. Usually searching for fish in the upper 20 metres of the sea, it can however, dive very deep and has even been spotted by a submersible operating hundreds of metres down. Only coming to shore to breed, on land it stands upright just like other auks.

**Guillemot** - The Guillemot is a medium-sized auk that breeds in tightly packed colonies on perilous ledges, cliff tops and rocky outcrops around the Norfolk coast. In May and June, female Guillemots will lay a single egg; once the chick is three weeks old, it will dramatically plunge into the sea with its father, who will care for it in the seawater until it is independent. Guillemots eat fish, crustaceans and molluscs, diving into the water and swimming after their prey.

**Cormorants** - Cormorants are large, black water birds. They feed on fish, which they catch with their long, hook-tipped bills while swimming underwater. Cormorants nest on low cliffs around the Norfolk coasts, or in colonies in trees on lakes and flooded gravel pits. Cormorants can often be spotted perched on a rock or bank with their wings held out. In this stance, they are able to dry their feathers off which are not waterproof.

**Fulmars** - Fulmars are members of a group of birds known as 'tubenoses', or 'petrels', which includes both giant Albatrosses and tiny Storm Petrels. They are found all around the Norfolk coast, nesting in colonies on cliffs or flocking to feed out at sea. Next, if you are ready, we will all go a Wading…

# Norfolk Wildlife

# Wading Birds in Norfolk

The wading birds that live, wade and thrive on sandy beaches, rivers, broads and the marshes of Norfolk.

**Snipe** - A medium-sized wader, the Snipe lives in marshes, wet grassland and moorlands, where it nests in simple scrapes. It uses its long, probing bill to find insects, earthworms and crustaceans in the mud, typically swallowing prey whole. During the breeding season, males can be heard making a unique 'drumming' sound as their tail feathers vibrate in the wind as they perform their aerial courtship displays.

**Woodcock** - A fairly large, short-legged wading bird, the Woodcock lives in woodlands and on heath-lands where its mottled plumage provides it with excellent camouflage as it probes around the ground for earthworms and beetles to eat. Norfolk's Woodcock are mostly residents, but are joined in the winter by other woodcock's from Finland and Russia.

**Curlew** - The Curlew is a very large, tall wader, about the same size as a female Pheasant. Its haunting display call ('cur-lee') is unmistakable and can be heard from February through to July on its breeding grounds which are the wet grasslands, farmland, heath and the moorlands of Norfolk. From July onwards, coastal numbers start to build up, peaking in January.

**Ringed Plover** - A small, rotund wader, the Ringed Plover nests on bare gravel, shingle and sand on the Norfolk coast and around flooded gravel pits and reservoirs. Like other plovers, it forages for invertebrates and crustaceans in a particular way: standing and watching, running forward, pecking, then standing still again. The Ringed Plover tempts underground prey to the surface by ' foot-trembling': tapping its feet fast on the ground to mimic raindrops…

# Norfolk Wildlife

## Wading Birds in Norfolk

**Avocet** - A scarce wading bird, the Avocet is about the same size as an Oystercatcher, but much more slender. It feeds on aquatic insects, worms and crustaceans, which it finds by sweeping its bill from side-to-side in shallow water. It is often seen on estuaries and mud-flats at the Norfolk coast where it breeds on exposed mud banks in a dug-out scrape.

**Oystercatcher** - The Oystercatcher is a very noisy wading bird with a loud peeping call. On the Norfolk coast, it specialises in eating shellfish, particularly cockles and mussels, which it either prises or hammers open with its strong, flattened bill. Originally a coastal species, the Oystercatcher has moved further inland over the last 50 years to breed on the Norfolk Broads.

**Coot** - A familiar bird on the Norfolk wetlands, the Coot is often seen on park lakes, ponds and rivers. It spends more of its time on the water than its relative, the Moorhen, and will dive to catch small invertebrates. Unlike ducks, Coots will bring their catch to the surface before eating it, leading to squabbles over food. Coots breed in spring, laying between six and nine eggs in nests made among emergent vegetation. Coot chicks are black with orange fluff around the face and body; they are independent within two months of hatching.

**Moorhen** - A familiar bird on the Norfolk wetlands, the Moorhen is often seen on park lakes, ponds and rivers. It spends more of its time out of the water than its relative, the Coot, and even climbs trees. Moorhens are omnivores, eating everything from snails and insects to small fish and berries. In the water below the wading birds are the amphibians and after putting your binoculars back in there case that is who we are going to be focusing on next…

# Norfolk Wildlife

## The Amphibians of Norfolk

Below are the amphibians that live and thrive in the rivers and broads of Norfolk.

**Common Frog** - Common frogs are amphibians, breeding in ponds during the spring and spending much of the rest of the year feeding in woodland, gardens, hedgerows and grassland. They are familiar inhabitants of Norfolk garden ponds, where they lay their eggs in big 'rafts' of spawn. They feed on a variety of invertebrates and even smaller amphibians.

**Natterjack Toad** - Smaller than the common toad, the natterjack toad is very rare. This amphibian breeds in warm, shallow pools on sand dunes and sandy heaths in just a handful of special places in Norfolk. Natterjack toads are mainly nocturnal; in the spring, the males all sing together at night to attract females and their calls can be heard up to a mile away!

**Common Toad** - Common toads are amphibians, breeding in ponds during the spring and spending much of the rest of the year feeding in woodland, gardens, hedgerows and grassland. They are famous for their mass migrations back to their breeding ponds on the first warm, damp evenings of the year, often around St. Valentine's Day. Common toads tend to breed in larger, deeper ponds than common frogs, but still frequent Norfolk gardens. They hibernate over winter, often under log piles, stones or even in old flower pots!

**Newts** - Newts are amphibians, breeding in ponds during the spring and spending most of the rest of the year feeding on invertebrates in woodland, hedgerows, marshes and grassland. They hibernate underground, among tree roots and in old walls. Next with binoculars back at the ready we will focus on the waterfowl of Norfolk…

# Norfolk Wildlife

## The Waterfowl of Norfolk

Below are the waterfowl that live, swim and thrive in the wet lands of Norfolk.

**Eider** - Eiders are relatively large sea ducks that nest in colonies around the Norfolk coasts. Once hatched, the chicks often gather together in a large 'crèche' looked after by a number of females.

**Mallard** - The Mallard is the most familiar sight in Norfolk at our local parks and village ponds, and are often very tame, being fed by the public regularly.

**Mute Swan** - The Mute Swan is one of the most familiar birds seen in Norfolk, its long, curved neck and graceful glide a regular sight on our waterways. Mute Swans feed on plants, particularly waterweed. They usually mate for life, but some will have numerous partner.

**Great White Egret** - Compared to the now familiar little egret, the great white egret is enormous, almost as large as a grey heron. Some now winter in Norfolk. Visiting birds can be found in all kinds of wetland habitats, even farmland ditches! They stand in shallow water, waiting for fish, insects and amphibians to approach, then spear them with their dagger-like bill.

**Spoonbill** - The spoonbill is a relative of the ibises, a group of long-legged birds with curved bills. Almost as big as a grey heron, the spoonbill feeds on shrimps and other aquatic invertebrates which it catches while sweeping its bizarre, spoon-shaped bill from side to side in the water. Seen most regularly in Norfolk at coastal sites, it mainly breeds in southern Europe and North Africa and in India and China. In recent years breeding birds have also become established in Norfolk.

**Little Egret** - The Little Egret is a small, white heron that feeds on small fish and crustaceans. Once a very rare visitor from the Mediterranean, Little Egrets are now an almost common sight around the Norfolk coast.

**Grey Heron** - A tall, often solitary bird, the Grey Heron is one of Norfolk's most familiar birds. It feeds mainly on fish, but also eats small mammals (even Moles!), water birds and Crayfish. It is often seen standing stock-still in the shallow waters of lakes, rivers and ponds, patiently hunting fish that flit about below the surface. It visits ornamental ponds, looking for an easy meal.

**Bittern** - A rare and shy heron, the Bittern spends almost all its time hidden away in large reed beds, where it feeds on eels and other fish. It is has wonderfully camouflaged plumage, helping it to blend in with the Norfolk reeds. It can also stand motionless for long periods to avoid detection. Raising our binoculars to our eyes we will next meet the swooping Norfolk birds of prey…

# Norfolk Wildlife

## The Birds of Prey of Norfolk

Below are the birds of prey that hunt, swoop and thrive in the skies of Norfolk.

**Barn Owl** - The barn owl has a mottled silver-grey and buff back, and a pure white underside. It has a distinctive heart-shaped, white face, and black eyes.

**Little Owl** - Although mainly nocturnal, the little owl can be spotted in the day hunting invertebrates (especially worms), small mammals, reptiles, amphibians and small birds.

**Tawny Owl** - The tawny owl is our largest common owl and is known for making the familiar twit-twoo owl call during the night and early hours.

**Kestrel** - The Kestrel is a little smaller than a Feral Pigeon and can be found in all kinds of habitats, from open countryside to towns and villages. They nest in holes in trees, old buildings and abandoned Crows' nests, laying between four and five eggs. When they hatch, both parents help to feed the young chicks.

**Sparrow hawk** - The Sparrow hawk is one of our smallest birds of prey, the male being somewhere between a Blackbird and a Collared Dove in size. The female is larger, up to the size of a Feral Pigeon. Sparrow hawks are excellent bird hunters, catching small species like finches, sparrows and tits; sometimes they ambush their prey from a perch, while other times they may fly low, suddenly changing direction to fool it's prey.

**Buzzard** - Until recently, the Buzzard was only found in the north and west of the country due to severe population declines. Over the last couple of decades, however, it has been doing very well and can now be found almost everywhere in Norfolk. Buzzards eat small birds, mammals and carrion, but will also eat large insects and earthworms when prey is in short supply.

**Red Kite** - The Red Kite is a large, graceful bird of prey, it soars over woods and open areas in Norfolk, its distinctive shape and 'mewing' calls making it easy to identify. Red Kites were routinely persecuted as hunters of game and domestic animals, but they are in fact scavengers, eating carrion and scraps, and taking only small prey like rabbits. Holding on tightly to our binoculars we will next go from the hunter to being the hunted…

# Norfolk Wildlife

## The Game Birds of Norfolk

Below are the game birds that live and hopefully thrive in Norfolk.

**Quail** - The Quail is a migratory species of game bird, travelling as far south as Africa for the winter, then returning to Norfolk to breed in late spring. Farmland birds, they spend most of their time on the floor, hidden in grass or in cereal fields. **Pheasant** - A very familiar game bird, the Pheasant is large and colourful, and has a long tail. Common in farmland and woodland throughout Norfolk, the males' loud, sharp, croaking call can be heard resonating through the countryside before the bird is actually seen. Pheasants eat seeds, berries, leaves and insects; they roost in trees and can form flocks in winter.

**Grey Partridge** - A plump, round game bird, the Grey Partridge is quite common in parts of Norfolk, but is becoming scarce around much of the country. A farmland bird, it feeds on seeds, leaves and small invertebrates. When disturbed, it prefers to run instead of fly, but will fly low to the ground if necessary. It breeds in open scrub and farmland, close to hedges or other vegetation, laying its eggs on the ground in a grass-lined scrape.

**Red-Legged Partridge** - A plump, round game bird, the Red-legged Partridge is common on Norfolk farmland, where it feeds on seeds, leaves and small invertebrates. When disturbed, it prefers to run instead of fly, but will fly short distances if necessary. It breeds in open scrub and farmland, laying its eggs on the ground. Now we come to the main reason why you need your binoculars with you. Because as we leave the game birds behind and move into the final section of Norfolk Wildlife you will need them so you can see what other bird-watching delights await you in the beautiful Norfolk countryside. Welcome to the world of birds!…

# Norfolk Wildlife

## Bird Watching in Norfolk

To complete our journey through the wildlife of Norfolk we will, in this last section, read about many of the birds that visit the Norfolk fields, gardens and bring so much joy to all bird-watchers. The birds not only bring movement, colours and song to the hedgerows, woods, fields and gardens of Norfolk but also mark the seasons. The Robin in the holly at Christmas time and the first swallow arriving in the spring and the little Jenny Wren busily collecting food for her young in the summer in our Norfolk garden.

**Collared Dove** - The Collared Dove is a small pigeon found on farmland and in woodland, parks and gardens across Norfolk. **Turtle Dove** - The Turtle Dove is a small pigeon, just a little bit smaller than Collared Dove. **Stock Dove** - The Stock Dove is a medium-sized pigeon that nests in holes in trees and in farm buildings in Norfolk. **Wood pigeon** - Our largest and most common pigeon, the wood pigeon is a familiar bird in Norfolk gardens, parks, woodlands and farmlands. **Kingfisher** - The Kingfisher is a colourful bird of rivers and streams. It can be spotted sitting quietly on low-hanging branches over the water, suddenly diving in to catch a small fish. **Cuckoo** - About the size of a Collared Dove. The Cuckoo is famous for laying its eggs in other birds' nests and fooling them into raising its young. **Lesser Spotted Woodpecker** - The Lesser Spotted Woodpecker is the smallest and least common of the UK's three species of woodpecker. **Green Woodpecker** - The Green Woodpecker is the largest of the UK's woodpeckers. It nests in holes that it excavates in trees in broad-leaved woodlands, orchards, large parks and gardens. **Great Spotted Woodpecker** - The Great Spotted Woodpecker is a medium-sized woodpecker. It nests in holes that it excavates in trees in broad-leaved woodlands, large parks and gardens. **Swallow** - The Swallow, or 'Barn Swallow', is a summer visitor to Norfolk. It builds mud and straw nests on ledges, often in farm buildings and outhouses, or under the eaves of houses. **House Martin** - A summer visitor and it builds mud nests, sometimes in small colonies, under ledges, on cliffs and, as their name suggests, under the eaves of houses. **Sand Martin** - The Sand Martin nests in colonies, digging burrows in steep, sandy cliffs, usually around water, and is commonly found on wetland sites. **Swift** - The swift with long, curved wings originally nesting on cliffs and in holes in trees, it now mainly nests in buildings, such as churches, and is particularly common in older parts of Norfolk towns…

# Norfolk Wildlife

## Bird Watching in Norfolk

**Tree Sparrow** - The Tree Sparrow is a scarce bird on Norfolk farmland, hedgerows and woodland edges. Tree Sparrows mate for life; they nest in holes in trees. **House Sparrow** - The House Sparrow is an opportunistic bird of villages, towns, parks, gardens and farmland. They live in colonies and nest in holes or crevices in buildings, among Ivy or other bushes, and in nest boxes. **Dunnock** - The Dunnock is a small bird, about the size of a Robin, which is common in Norfolk gardens, parks, hedgerows, scrub and along woodland edges. They nest in hedges or shrubs, laying up to five eggs. **Grey Wagtail** - The Grey Wagtail can be spotted in Norfolk farmyards and even in towns. They nest near the water in hollows and crevices lined with moss and twigs. **Yellow Wagtail** - The Yellow Wagtail likes damp marshes, meadows and farmland. Wagtails nest on the ground or in long grass, using plants, grasses and stems to build a cup-shape which they line with fur. **Pied Wagtail** - The Pied Wagtail is often seen in Norfolk villages and towns, dashing across lawns, roads and car parks while wagging its long tail up and down. They flock together at warm roost sites like reed beds and sewage works or trees and bushes in the city centre. **Meadow Pipit** - The Meadow Pipit is a common nesting bird in heath-land and rough grassland. **Rock Pipit** - The Rock Pipit lives on rocky beaches and feeds on seeds, small molluscs and invertebrates. **Woodlark** - The secretive Woodlark favours open, dry habitats with short grasses. Moves to farmland stubbles for the autumn and early winter. **Skylark** - Male Skylarks can be spotted rising almost vertically from Norfolk farmland, grassland, salt marshes and moorland. They sing from perches, such as fence posts or large rocks. **Wren** - The diminutive wren (or the Jenny Wren as she is known in Norfolk) can be found in almost any habitat where there are insects to eat and bushes or rock crevices in which to build their domed nest out of moss and twigs. **Robin** - Robins regularly visit our Norfolk garden. Robins are also common in parks, scrub and woodland, making their presence known with a loud, territorial song. They sing from prominent perches right through the winter and are fiercely territorial…

# Norfolk Wildlife

## Bird Watching in Norfolk

**Blackbird** - The melodious blackbird is a common sight in our Norfolk gardens, parks and woodland. Blackbirds are especially fond of feeding on our lawn and can be seen with their heads cocked to one side, listening for earthworms. **Starling** - The starling spend a lot of their time in large flocks, roosting and performing sweeping, aerial displays. They make untidy nests in holes in trees or in buildings. **Tree-Creeper** - The Tree-creeper climbs up trees in a spiral around the trunk, feeding on insects and spiders that they find in crevices in the bark. **Nuthatch** - The Nuthatch has a short tail, large head and a woodpecker-like bill. Nuthatches climb up and down tree trunks in mature Norfolk woods and parklands. **Spotted Flycatcher** - The Spotted Flycatcher has a relatively long tail, which it flicks while it sits patiently on a perch waiting for a chance to fly out and catch its insect-prey in mid-air. **Stonechat** - The Stonechat is a little smaller than a Robin. It has a big head and short tail. It can frequently be seen sitting on the top of gorse bushes, flicking its wings and making a call like two small stones being hit together. **Nightingale** - The Nightingale is about the same size as a Robin. They nest in dense scrub, from where they sing their famously beautiful melodies throughout the day and also at night. **Fieldfare** - Fieldfare's are sociable birds and can be seen in flocks of more than 200 birds roaming through the countryside. **Redwing** - The Redwing is a small thrush that can be spotted in hedgerows, orchards, parks and gardens. **Mistle Thrush** - The Mistle Thrush is a large songbird and gets its common name from its love of Mistletoe. **Song Thrush** - The Song Thrush is commonly found in parks and gardens, woodland. Living up to its common name, it has a beautiful, loud song with repeating phrases. **Firecrest** - The Firecrest is found in coniferous forests and woods in Norfolk. **Chiffchaff** - The Chiffchaff sings its name out loud in a simple 'chiff chaff chiff chaff' song, which it performs from the tree canopy. **Willow Warbler** - The Willow Warbler is a slim, delicate bird of woodland, scrub, parks and gardens. It can be heard singing a melodious, warbling song from the tree canopy…

# Norfolk Wildlife

# Bird Watching in Norfolk

**Cetti's Warbler** - The Cetti's Warbler is found in Norfolk willow scrub, marshes and nettle beds. **Reed Warbler** - The Reed Warbler is found in the reed beds, and rivers and is a summer visitor to the UK. **Sedge Warbler** - The Sedge Warbler is found in the marshes, reed beds and wetlands. It is a great mimic and never singing the same song twice. **Lesser Whitethroat** - Is a medium-sized warbler of dense scrub and woodland edges. It is easily located by its rattling, monotonous song. **Whitethroat** - Is a long-tailed warbler of grassland, scrub and hedgerows. It is a summer visitor to Norfolk. **Garden Warbler** - Found in the woodland and tall scrub. A summer visitor around the east coast up until September. **Blackcap** - Is found in woodland and tall scrub, but also in gardens, particularly during the winter. They nest in hedges or brambles. **Goldcrest** - Is found in conifer woodland, scrub, park's and gardens. They are often found in bushes on sand dunes. It is our smallest songbird. **Marsh Tit** - Is a small, mainly brown bird, with a shiny black cap, neat black bib and pale belly. Marsh tits are most often found in broadleaf woodland, copses, park's and in gardens. **Willow Tit** - The willow tit is found in wet woodland, wetlands, bog's and around gravel pits. They use their small bills to excavate nest holes in decaying wood. **Long-tailed Tit** - The long-tailed tit is a tiny bird found in hedgerows, woodland, parks and gardens. They often visit our garden bird table and feeders. **Coal Tit** - The coal tit is a small tit of coniferous woodland, although it can be found in parks and gardens. They also visit our bird table and feeders. **Blue Tit** - Smaller than the great tit, the blue tit is also a bird of woodland, parks and gardens. They also visit our bird table and feeders. **Great Tit** - The largest of the UK's tits, the great tit is a bird found in woodland, parks and gardens. It nests in holes in trees but also visit our bird table and feeders. **Raven** - The Raven is a massive crow found in the wooded areas of Norfolk where it feeds on carrion. **Crow** - Is completely black and makes a hoarse, cawing sound found on farmland and grassland and are mostly solitary. **Rook** - The Rook gathers in large colonies known as 'rookeries'; they nest in the trees near our Norfolk village and make a great sight and noise when they arrive and leave their rookeries…

# Norfolk Wildlife

# Bird Watching in Norfolk

**Jackdaw** - The Jackdaw is a bird of woodland, parkland, coasts and urban areas. It nests in holes in trees, and on cliffs and buildings. **Jay** - The Jay is a brightly coloured crow that can be found in woodland, parks and gardens. **Magpie** - The Magpie is the source of much myth and legend: 'one for sorrow, two for a joy...' is a rhyme that many children learn. They are famous for collecting all kinds of objects, particularly anything shiny, to decorate their nest. **Corn Bunting** - A streaky brown bird of hedgerows and farmland. Their song that sounds just like a jangling set of keys. **Yellowhammer** - A bright yellow bird of woodland edges, hedgerows, heath and farmland. They are often seen perched on top of bushes. **Reed Bunting** - found in reed beds, wetlands and farmland. **Common Crossbill** - Found in conifer woodlands, so-named for its bizarre, cross-tipped bill, which it uses to lever out and eat the seeds from pine cones. **Bullfinch** - The Bullfinch feeds on buds and fruit in woodlands, hedgerows, parklands, gardens and orchards. Beautiful, easy to tame and skilful at mimicry, it was often taken as a cage-bird in times past. **Siskin** - The Siskin is a common, small finch of conifer woodlands and some mixed woods. They often come into our garden to feed and collect seeds. **Goldfinch** - The goldfinch is a striking, small finch of gardens, parks, woodland, heath-land and farmland. They also often come into our garden to feed and collect seeds. **Greenfinch** - The Greenfinch is a large finch of gardens, parks, woodland and farmland. They to come into our garden to feed and collect seeds. **Lesser Redpoll** - The Lesser Redpoll is a small finch of mixed woodland, birch scrub and wet woodland. It is now becoming a more common garden visitor. **Linnet** - The Linnet is found on heath-land, scrub and farmland. They were once popular cage birds due to their melodious song. **Chaffinch** - The chaffinch is a very common, sparrow-sized finch in gardens, woodland, parks and farmland. They visit our garden and prefer to hop about on the ground, lawn and under our hedge. Chaffinches are present all the year round and they have a loud and pleasant song. So as the rainbow falls on the Norfolk harvest and the birds have gone to bed sadly we have come to the end of our quest to meet the wildlife of Norfolk. In the next chapter we will enjoy **Norfolk in Colour**…

# Norfolk in Colour

Norfolk windmills

# Norfolk in Colour

The beautiful City of Norwich

# Norfolk in Colour

Beach huts and flowers in the Norfolk landscape

# Norfolk in Colour

Boats and a seaside pier in Norfolk

# Norfolk in Colour

Parade of beach huts and all out at Norwich cathedral

# Norfolk in Colour

All tied up! and all alone again!

# Norfolk in Colour

An ideal day on the Norfolk Broads! and windmill on the broads

# Norfolk in Colour

The Blakeney Hotel and the gates are shut at Dereham

# Norfolk in Colour

Blowing in the wind and the beach at Brancaster

# Norfolk in Colour

Burnham Overy Staithe harbour and sunset on Burnham Overy Staithe

# Norfolk in Colour

Cley windmill reed marshes and evening light in Norwich

# Norfolk in Colour

The beach at Cromer and the pier at Cromer

# Norfolk in Colour

Gressenhall museum working horses and the lighthouse at Happisburgh

# Norfolk in Colour

High and dry at Wells and a Kingfisher

# Norfolk in Colour

The mill at Hunsett and love is in the air!

# Norfolk in Colour

Pebbles on the beach at Heacham and windmill in the reeds!

# Norfolk in Colour

Boats at Morston and the beach at Holkham

# Norfolk in Colour

Windmill and a red fox in the reeds!

# Norfolk in Colour

Boats ready on the ramp at Sheringham and going out to sea!

# Norfolk in Colour

The reed cutter and the wind turbines at Scroby Sands!

I hope you have enjoyed seeing Norfolk in colour. Now in the last chapter of this book, we will see some pictures taken from our family album of memories, scanned onto my computer and then re-produced in the chapter that is called - "Our Norfolk Snaps"…

# Our Norfolk Snaps

## Our Snaps Taken in Norfolk

In this the last chapter of my Norfolk book I have included a few snaps from our family album of photographs showing the many happy times that we have had in the wonderful County of Norfolk over the years.

Susie building a boat in the sand on Hunstanton beach

Olivia sitting in the boat that Susie built

## Our Norfolk Snaps

Ginny, Susie and our dogs walking in Shouldham Warren woods,
field of red poppies, Alan aged 1 in Earlham Park, Susie on her trick long ago
and Susie and Alan in 1993

# Our Norfolk Snaps

Ginny in shades on Cromer beach

Susie in shades on Old Hunstanton beach

## Our Norfolk Snaps

Susie and Ginny walking the dogs in Shouldham Warren, the signpost, Susie at Wells Next the Sea, Frank, Dad and me at North Creake and Beryl, Joyce with Nanny Dorrington on a night out!

# Our Norfolk Snaps

My Mandy and Paul happy in their Norfolk home

Mandy and Adrian's wedding day, Phyllis and Dennis and Phyllis and Mum

# Our Norfolk Snaps

Alan (me) and my sister Doreen at Mandy's wedding

The Massen family

## Our Norfolk Snaps

Alan in our garden, Susie enjoying the sun, a field of rape seed flowers and the open doorway to a Norfolk cliff top lighthouse

# Our Norfolk Snaps

Red Deer at Snettisham Park

Alan and Ginny at Wells Next the Sea

# Our Norfolk Snaps

Andy and Lynn at our Norfolk home, Susie, Andy, Lynn and the dogs at their Sheffield home, Christmas comes to Shouldham Warren and the light through the trees at the Warren

# Our Norfolk Snaps

Susie and Alan on holiday in Mousehole Cornwall, a Norfolk lighthouse and flowers in our Norfolk garden

## Our Norfolk Snaps

Ginny taking snaps and when we were puppies by Charlie and Poppy

## Our Norfolk Snaps

Thrush in our garden, Susie and Alan at the Troulos Bay Hotel on Skiathos, a Norfolk windmill, our local bus and Shouldham villages against the quarry!

# Our Norfolk Snaps

Susie in our garden in the Norfolk sunshine with our dog Poppy
and Swan in the river at Norwich

# Our Norfolk Snaps

Sunset on the Norfolk coast and on the Norfolk Broads

## Our Norfolk Snaps

Alan in our garden, Ginny and Alan at Thrigby Hall, wind turbines off the coast Shouldham village green and a Norfolk windmill

# Our Norfolk Snaps

Norfolk windmill and walking on a Norfolk beach

# Our Norfolk Snaps

A little tern taking a fish supper home, Mandy on her Norwich wedding day, Adrian and Mandy on holiday and Mum, Dad, Phyllis, Christopher and Julie in the Norfolk fresh air many years ago!

## Our Norfolk Snaps

Mushroom fungus growing in Shouldham Warren

# Our Norfolk Snaps

A Norfolk seaside pier, a seal and Lou, Gerard with baby Olivia on the beach

## Our Norfolk Snaps

Our dogs Charlie and Poppy, flowers in our garden, Alan all at sea and Olivia enjoying the paddling pool in our Norfolk garden

# Our Norfolk Snaps

The beautiful Norfolk coast and Alan is waving goodbye to you from Norfolk

Norfolk, like many other counties, has benefited greatly from tourism since the beginning of the Great British Summer Holiday way back in 1871. Many of our resorts happily cope with many thousands of working families coming to spend their summer holidays with them every year. I hope my book will encouraged you to come and join us in this wonderful county. It is now time for us to part and sadly leave the county of Norfolk behind us. I hope that you have enjoyed seeing our coast, inland towns, villages, the wildlife, the broads as well as many other Norfolk highlights featured in this book. I hope to see you real soon in the County of my Birth. Until then keep well, be happy and keep on smiling!…

# Acknowledgement

To all the people of Norfolk, my family and friends that are mentioned or illustrated in this book that have enriched my life immeasurably, I wish to express my gratitude. I would especially like to thank my publisher Rainbow Publications UK for publishing my books. A special mention must also go to my late father Arthur, my late mother Edith, and my late son Paul who all gave me unconditional love and support. Their memory helps to inspire me to observe, write, garden and paint everyday. Finally I wish to thank my lovely wife Susie, for without someone to share life's journey with and help you fully enjoy the things you see around you your life would be very poor indeed! Last of all, like my hero Lord Nelson said, I would just like to say to everyone reading this book:

## "I am very proud to be AN OLD NORFOLK BOY"

This year, 2020, I will have reached more than seventy years of age so I have decided to make this book the last one that I write. Yes I know that I have said this before but this really is it so:

## Anyway All Good things must come to an end so It's Goodbye from Norfolk and It's Goodbye from Me!

As you can see there really is a pot of gold at the end of a rainbow and it is called **NORFOLK** so hurry up and visit us real soon.

Just before we leave my Norfolk I would like to finish by dedicating this book to all those people worldwide who have lost loved ones during the recent terrible Coronavirus pandemic of 2020. All those who have left us will always be remembered and live on in our hearts and minds as we remember all of the love, support and smiles that they shared with us during their lifetimes. I would also like to thank the wonderful, dedicated and brave doctors, nurses and all of the other essential workers who put their own lives at risk to help others during this tragedy. Their bravery has been an inspiration to us all during this awful time and we thank each and to every one of them.

**THANK YOU**...

Copyright © 2020 Alan R. Massen

# The End

www.ingramcontent.com/pod-product-compliance
Lightning Source LLC
Chambersburg PA
CBHW061925290426
44113CB00024B/2826

# Transactions
## of the
## American Philosophical Society
Held at Philadelphia
For Promoting Useful Knowledge
Volume 89, Pt. 6

## THE COSMIC INVENTOR

## REGINALD AUBREY FESSENDEN
## (1866-1932)

FREDERICK SEITZ
Rockefeller University

American Philosophical Society
Independence Square ◆ Philadelphia
1999

Copyright © 1999 by the American Philosophical Society for its *Transactions* series, Vol. 89, Pt. 6. All rights reserved.

ISBN: 0-87169-896-X
US ISSN:0065-9746

Library of Congress Cataloging-in-Publication Data

Seitz, Frederick, 1911-
    The cosmic inventor: Reginald Aubrey Fessenden (1866-1932) / Frederick Seitz.
  p. cm. (Transactions of the American Philosophical Society; v. 89, pt. 6)
    ISBN 0-87169-896-X (pbk.)
    1. Fessenden, Reginald Aubrey, 1866-1932. 2. Electric engineers--United States--Biography. 3. Inventors--United States--Biography. I. Title. II. Series.

TK140.F48 S45 1999
621.3'092--dc21
[B]
                                        99-057137